Human Remains
Curation, Reburial and Repatriation

Working with human remains raises a whole host of ethical issues, from how the remains are used to how and where they are stored. Over recent years, attitudes towards repatriation and reburial have changed considerably and there are now laws in many countries to facilitate or compel the return of remains to claimant communities. Such changes have also brought about new ways of working with and caring for human remains, while enabling their ongoing use in research projects. This has often meant a re-evaluation of working practices for both the curation of remains and in providing access to them. This volume looks at the issues and difficulties inherent in holding human remains with global origins, and how diverse institutions and countries have tackled these issues. It is essential reading for advanced students in biological anthropology, museum studies, archaeology and anthropology, as well as museum curators, researchers and other professionals.

Margaret Clegg is an honorary senior research associate at University College London and was formerly head of the Human Remains Unit of the Natural History Museum in London. She is a leading expert on the issue of repatriation of human remains, and her research also focuses on the archaeological evidence for hominin cognition and the evolution of modern human growth and development, including modern human morphological variation. She is a member of the American Association of Physical Anthropologists (AAPA), British Association of Biological Anthropology and Osteoarchaeology (BABAO) and a variety of advisory panels including the steering committee of the Advisory Panel on the Archaeology of Burials in England (APABE).

Cambridge Texts in Human Bioarcheology and Osteoarchaeology

Series Editor

Piers Mitchell
University of Cambridge

Cambridge Texts in Human Bioarchaeology and Osteoarchaeology provide practical guides for Masters level students as well as advanced undergraduate students, and field archaeologists and academics who wish to learn more about topics outside their own area of expertise. These concise and affordable texts will provide more in-depth coverage of all the core topics in bioarchaeology and those which most capture students' imaginations.

Forthcoming titles
Statistical Methods for Biological Anthropology
Forensic Anthropology
Mummies of the World
Imaging in Human Bioarcheology: Research and Practice

Human Remains

Curation, Reburial and Repatriation

Margaret Clegg
University College London

CAMBRIDGE
UNIVERSITY PRESS

University Printing House, Cambridge CB2 8BS, United Kingdom

One Liberty Plaza, 20th Floor, New York, NY 10006, USA

477 Williamstown Road, Port Melbourne, VIC 3207, Australia

314–321, 3rd Floor, Plot 3, Splendor Forum, Jasola District Centre,
New Delhi – 110025, India

79 Anson Road, #06–04/06, Singapore 079906

Cambridge University Press is part of the University of Cambridge.

It furthers the University's mission by disseminating knowledge in the pursuit of
education, learning, and research at the highest international levels of excellence.

www.cambridge.org
Information on this title: www.cambridge.org/9781107098381
DOI: 10.1017/9781316161654

© Margaret Clegg 2020

First published 2020

Printed in the United Kingdom by TJ International Ltd, Padstow Cornwall

A catalogue record for this publication is available from the British Library.

Library of Congress Cataloging-in-Publication Data
Names: Clegg, Margaret, author.
Title: Human remains : curation, reburial and repatriation / Margaret Clegg, University College
 London.
Description: Cambridge, United Kingdom ; New York, NY, Cambridge University Press, 2020. |
 Series: Cambridge texts in human bioarchaeology and osteoarchaeology | Includes
 bibliographical references and index.
Identifiers: LCCN 2019038261 (print) | LCCN 2019038262 (ebook) | ISBN 9781107098381
 (hardback) | ISBN 9781107485433 (paperback) | ISBN 9781316161654 (epub)
Subjects: LCSH: Human remains (Archaeology)–History. | Archaeology–Research. |
 Human remains (Archaeology)–Repatriation. | Human remains (Archaeology)–Moral and
 ethical aspects.
Classification: LCC CC79.5.H85 C54 2020 (print) | LCC CC79.5.H85 (ebook) | DDC 930.1–dc23
LC record available at https://lccn.loc.gov/2019038261
LC ebook record available at https://lccn.loc.gov/2019038262

ISBN 978-1-107-09838-1 Hardback
ISBN 978-1-107-48543-3 Paperback

Contents

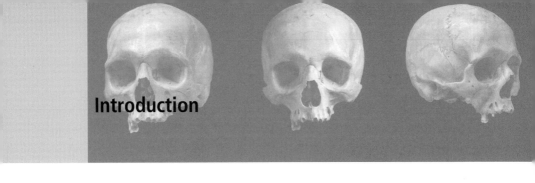

Introduction

Over the past thirty years considerable changes have occurred in attitudes towards the issue of repatriation and reburial. In many countries laws have been enacted to facilitate or compel the return of remains to claimant communities. These changes have also brought about new ways of working with human remains, not only when considering claims for return but also in the care of human remains more generally. These new approaches have meant a re-evaluation of working practices both for the curation of remains and in providing access to them. In the United Kingdom this has meant working within the legislative framework of the Human Tissue Act for National Museums and using the Department of Culture Media and Sport (DCMS) Guidance for Human Remains document for all repositories holding remains. Similar changes have, for example, been seen in the United States, New Zealand, Australia and South Africa. This volume will look at the issues and difficulties inherent in holding human remains with global origins and how diverse institutions and countries have tackled these issues. The volume has grown out of seminars, lectures and training courses I've given over the last twenty years. It is based on my own experiences of working with human remains in a wide variety of capacities from researcher and lecturer, to head of the Natural History Museum London's (NHM) Human Remains Unit. In the latter position I gained my experience of repatriation and all the issues and problems that this brings not only to museums but to the claimant communities too. Some chapters in the volume set the scene and help to give background information which can inform and enlighten the day-to-day practice of caring for human remains. Others are more practical and range from policy and procedures to provenancing human remains. The book is both how we as museum professionals and researchers got where we are both in the United Kingdom and in other parts of the Western tradition and a guide to both the main issues in human remains curation and the ethical and legal challenges involved. The volume is intended for those who are studying this area as part of their master's course, in both biological anthropology and disciplines such as museum studies, archaeology and anthropology, as well as those studying in disciplines in which museum practice or repatriation form a part. Museum professionals, such as curators and researchers with responsibilities in caring for human remains, particularly those beginning their career or with this responsibility as a new part of their job, may also find this volume useful. It may also be of value to indigenous communities or those advising them to gain an understanding of how museums outside their home country operate and the values and beliefs that may be prevalent in those countries. Many of the countries involved share a language but the worldview of both museum staff and the wider public may be very different to that in the claimant's home country.

The first chapter will give a historical background of why human remains are in museums in the first place and how they are currently used in research. The history of how and why remains came to be in museums is important in understanding the points of view of both the scientific and claimant communities. Many of the remains claimed for return were collected under conditions that today we would find abhorrent and unethical. It is important to understand this process, and that even when such remains seem legitimate in their acquisition in the past, those from former colonial countries have to be viewed through the unequal power dynamics at the time. Many researchers and even curators in the United Kingdom and other countries with museums that follow Western traditions have limited knowledge of the acquisition stories of the remains they care for or use in research. That knowledge can be shocking and change the perspective of the staff involved. This is most usually true for remains from outside the home country. In the United Kingdom, for example, this would mean remains from anywhere outside Europe; and in countries such as Australia, the United States and New Zealand, remains from elsewhere in the world even when these remains are from other indigenous communities. This information is often not included in the basic record of the remains or is outside the information passed from curator to curator. There is a belief from those outside museums, from researchers to indigenous communities, that the records within a museum are complete and fully accurate. The information is only as good as the original input; if anything is missing, altered or misrepresented then errors will exist, often without the current curators being aware of this.

In Chapter 2 the importance of human remains to science will be discussed. The main areas of research which involve human remains today will be detailed and a brief history of how remains have been incorporated into osteological studies in the past will be considered. One important aspect of the research undertaken today with human remains is that it often has real-world applications. Rather than purely being driven by academic curiosity which in the past looked for similarities and differences in remains, today researchers try to answer specific scientific questions. These can range from a better understanding of how children grow and develop, the effects of disease on bones, how our activities can shape our skeleton and looking for disease vectors and parasites in the remains themselves. The chapter will also look at the many different techniques used to examine remains, ranging from the well-known traditional methods to newer, more high-tech techniques. The chapter will give examples of the real-world issues that museum collections of human remains have addressed. It will also highlight problems inherent in working with human remains and the changes in attitude to providing access for scientific research that have occurred in recent years.

The legal aspects of human remains will be addressed Chapter 3, the most significant being the legal changes in the major countries involved in repatriation requests, and for those in European countries including the United Kingdom who deal with international requests for return. It will also look at how countries such as the United States that have a legal framework for national returns deal with international requests, and how these processes differ from those internal repatriations. This chapter also examines the more general laws pertaining to human remains, from burial laws to laws dealing with very recent remains concerning donations of bodies to science and medicine, licensing of the display of recent human remains and methods of acquisition by museums of the recently dead.

Working with human remains raises a host of ethical issues. Chapter 4 explores whether there is a universal ethical approach to human remains or whether this idea is so general as to be little more than broad statements. This chapter also provides a more general introduction to ethics. It is essential to have a good understanding of what this discipline actually means if curators and researchers are to act in truly ethical ways. In the literature discussing human remains there are only a few examples where general ethical principles are addressed. Most gloss over this aspect as if its understanding is a given. It is not. Many people, involved in working with remains or not, have at best a sketchy understanding of ethics yet we as academics and museum professionals are expected to draw up ethical codes and statements which, if they are to be more than a box-ticking exercise, must be based on a firm understanding.

Modern best practice in caring for human remains will be explored in Chapter 5. This chapter will give the context of the various guidance documents produced in different countries. Whether the country in question has one rule for all remains or whether remains are treated differently depending on differing circumstances: for example, the age of the remains, broadly the recently dead or the ancient dead, the origin of the remains and the usage of the remains. The processes needed to consider in respect of curation for remains that are claimed for return will also be considered here.

In addition, the volume looks at whether it is possible to take account of other belief systems when caring for remains and how this might work. Chapter 6 will give examples of how this has been attempted and explore what taking account of other beliefs might mean in the future. This is important if collaborative research is to be undertaken with indigenous communities.

The history of the repatriation movements in the major claimant countries will be detailed in Chapter 7. The drivers for why communities began to ask for return of remains are discussed and similarities and differences between distinct communities examined. Some landmark repatriation claims will be examined in this context and the role of third parties and activists will be examined. Major cases of returns from former colonial powers will also be examined to see how these were originally dealt with and what lessons were learnt.

In Chapter 8 current views on repatriation will be discussed, and what type of events can lead to a change in perspective. A case study based on my experiences while working at the NHM will be detailed to show the evolution of such a change.

One aspect that most museums and claimants would agree on is that it is important that only remains associated with the claimant community are considered for return. This highlights the importance of proper provenancing of remains, which is examined in Chapter 9. This chapter will look at the problems inherent in provenancing remains and how these problems may be overcome. It will also describe the approach taken in several major institutions in different countries to provenance and how a consensus view is beginning to emerge.

The issue of reburial versus keeping places is important, as keeping places allow for the possibility of future access to remains. These issues will be explored in Chapter 10. Many communities are now moving away from the view that they want to put remains beyond the reach of science and are beginning to understand how human remains can help both their own communities and the wider world. It also shows how the academic community has changed its views in general and is more able to respect the view of indigenous peoples when they want control of the remains.

Finally, Chapter 11 will look at collaboration between communities, museums, universities and other institutions. This collaboration is happening in many places and has roots in the beginnings of the repatriation movements. It is important that we move from indigenous people being the subject of a research project, exhibition or other activity to one in which they are full partners and in which their views hold equal weight with the others forming the team.

The book is not necessarily meant to be read in order but to be used as a beginning for understanding the issues surrounding human remains. Some parts may be better if read first. For example, to understand repatriation one needs to understand not only the current situation but also the history of how remains came to be in museums and other repositories. There is some repetition of information within the chapters and also references back to earlier and later chapters where relevant should the reader require more information. In addition each chapter has a set of questions which may help students to test their understanding, the answer to which will be found at the end of the book.

In this book I have used the term museum as a general catch-all for any institution which holds human remains. This is in keeping with Department of Culture Media and Sport in the United Kingdom (DCMS) Guidance on Human Remains which defines a museum as follows: the term refers to all museums any other institution permanently holding remains as collections.

In writing this book I have spoken to many people and read many articles, books and papers and I thank all of these people. However, there is a group of people that I have, over many years, had discussions with, help, advice and guidance from and encouragement in writing the book. Some are former colleagues, some co-authors and others members of indigenous communities, family and friends; some are many of those things at once. They are, in alphabetical order: Leslie Aiello, Sam Alberti, Amber Kiri Aranui, Edward Ayau, Jelena Bekvalac, Piotr Bienkowski, Wendy Birch, Heather Bonney, Megan Brickley, Jo Buckberry, Hallie Buckley, Jane Buikstra, Stacey Campton, Simon Chaplin, Helen Chatterjee, Carole Christophenson, Chris Clegg, Matthew Collins, Alan Cooper, Vince Copley, Vince Copley Jnr., Ned David, T. J. Ferguson, Cressida Fforde, Rob Foley, Myra Geisen, Te Herekiekie Haerehuka Herewini, Louise Humphreys, John Hunter, John Jackson, Malgosia Novak Kemp, Robert Kruszynsky, Marta Lahr, Dorothy Lippert, Emma Loban, Sarah Long, Norman Macleod, Angela Milner, Piers Mitchell, Nell Murphy, Lisa O'Sullivan, Steve Ousley, Norman Palmer, Sarah Parker, Kirk Perry, Carina Phillips, Mike Pickering, Innocent Pikirayi, Alexsandra Pretto, Rebecca Redfern, Daryl Rigney, Charlotte Roberts, Chris Rodgers, Fred Spoor, James Steele, Chris Stringer, Major Sumner, Nancy Tayles, Susan Thorpe, Micheal Westaway, Jennie White and Sonia Zakrzewsky. I would like to thank them all, and any I've forgotten. Any errors are my own.

1 A History of Human Remains in Museum and Other Collections

Human bones and particularly skulls have long fascinated people. Ancient and tribal peoples collected bones, skulls especially, as trophies and remembrances of enemies and family members (Haddon, 1890, 1904, 1932; Maschner & Reedy-Maschner, 2007; Bonney & Clegg, 2011). From these ancient collections to the eighteenth- and nineteenth-century cabinets of curiosities, which were never considered complete without at least one human skull, to the foundations of our modern collections and today's archaeological human remains collections, it is clear how important the remains even of enemies are to us. One of the atrocities of war is desecration of the dead to show contempt for those who are conquered (Wypijewski, 2006). Headhunting is nothing new (Bello et al., 2015), from Palaeolithic to twentieth-century skulls from genocides via Celtic and sacred relics, and we should keep this in mind when we consider the collection of human remains.

Ancient bones feature in many myths and legends, and even today stories and films make much of mummies' curses and terrible fates awaiting those who disturb the dead, especially the ancient dead (Day, 2006). This both fascinates and provides a frisson of fear, which is really rooted in our own cultural heritages; all cultures seem to have myths about the dangers of disturbing the dead (Day, 2006). Even today we expect that exhuming the dead will require permission from at least the state in the form of notifications or licences and, for the recently dead, from surviving family members (Márquez-Grant & Fibiger, 2011).

People all over the world and from many different cultures hold the dead and their remains in awe and respect. However, this does not mean that they all agree as to how these might be treated (Clegg & Long, 2015). This aspect of concern for the dead will be the subject of a later chapter. One question it does raise is how we view the dead collected long ago and often from far-away places that are currently held in modern museum collections. This is a complicated issue as the remains may be contemporary to the collection date or may be very ancient. The issue of the different categories of the dead will be examined in Chapter 4 and is deeply relevant to our current situation. However, to understand such issues we must first appreciate how these remains came to be collected and eventually became part of our museum, university and private collections. One might suppose that this was a modern issue but there is a long history of collecting and distributing human remains (Quigley, 2001). People in the past were not always as squeamish as many of us are today and viewing the dead and displaying the bones of ancestors and important people was more common than we might suppose. It is in part in this that our current collections have their roots.

1.1   The Ancients

From earliest times people have revered their dead relatives and even the bones of their enemies. There is evidence of intentional burial even beyond our own species, with deliberate burials being found perhaps as early as 300,000 years ago (Arsuaga *et al.*, 1997). One reason we have so many Neanderthal remains is because they intentionally buried their dead (Zorich, 2014). Many ancient cultures brought out the bones of the dead for ceremonies and to be venerated or even worshipped. Some of the earliest skulls have evidence of de-fleshing but do not show the classic signs of cannibalism (White *et al.*, 2003). The assumption here must be that these earlier cultures not only buried their dead but also had well-established mortuary processes, which de-fleshed bones immediately after death, perhaps for hygienic reasons, and also included the likelihood that the ancestral bones were open to view at least for a time. This latter view is supported by the positioning and weathering of the bones seen when they are excavated. For example, Neolithic bones show a pattern of weathering associated with regular exposure to the elements which suggests they were not permanently kept in the tomb or barrow (Robb *et al.*, 2015). Indeed, the way in which Neolithic burial mounds are set out suggests that bodies were actually on a journey, presumably into the next world (Robb *et al.*, 2015). The arrangement of the bones suggests that certain parts were more

Figure 1.1 Naturally mummified body from Egypt.
Credit: Print Collector/Contributor/Hulton Archive/Getty Images

important and that once bodies had become a collection of bones they were stored in very specific ways reminiscent of charnel houses or ossuaries in later times.

The ancient Egyptians so revered the dead that important or wealthy people were mummified. All levels of Egyptian society aspired to mummification and many individuals were either naturally or intentionally mummified. The Egyptians believed that this allowed them to be immortal and bring their bodies into the next life (Clarysse, 2011). The earliest mummies were all naturally mummified in the hot desert sand, which desiccated the body. If these bodies were found then they would look so lifelike that it would seem as if they were preserved for a reason (Figure 1.1). This inspired the Egyptians to find methods of preservation (Jones *et al.*, 2014), which became more complicated and therefore expensive and so became a status symbol.

The Celtic tribes in Britain and Europe were headhunters and took the heads of their enemies in battle and kept them (Cunliffe, 1988). The heads were usually stored in niches around the doors of houses or attached to their horses' manes or their chariots (Cunliffe, 1988). This may have been to show

how many men a warrior had killed and so prove his bravery or, if around the doorway, might have been designed to protect the house and help keep those who lived there safe by warning any who visited that if they showed themselves to be enemies there would be no mercy. This style of headhunting is widespread in many cultures and although the storage method may be slightly different, the reasons given by present-day or at least fairly recent headhunters are very similar to those we surmise for the past (Janes, 2005).

1.2   Saints and Sinners

Relics from saints were always part of the Christian tradition dating back to the very early days of Christianity (Ward, 2010). When people who were considered holy died then their bodies often had parts removed and given to other religious institutions or to kings, emperors and high-ranking nobles to bless and protect those individuals. At first this may have been a respectable trade but before long relics were produced more as a business than as a holy enterprise (Ward, 2010). Fragments of bone changed hands for vast sums of money and some saints had more fingers, toes and long bones than would be possible. This was well known in medieval times and it was often said that if all the pieces of the 'true' cross were real then Christ was crucified on a forest. The source of human bones in the medieval period was easy as churches regularly cleared their graveyards and placed the bones in charnel houses. Gravediggers and others living nearby were well placed to collect scattered bones and either make relics themselves or sell the bones on to those who did.

Many nobles, as well as religious institutions, had large collections of saints' bones, often preserved as relics in elaborate reliquaries, which were displayed and in the case of the religious houses could be viewed for a fee. This was a lucrative business and brought in much revenue for religious orders at the time. It was a contributory factor in the Reformation (Eire, 1986) and in earlier challenges to church authority, such as the Lollards in the thirteenth century (Birch, 2009). However, these collections in religious houses and royal palaces do mark a beginning of collecting human remains for display in a modern sense.

The holy were not the only people whose bones were displayed. The bones, particularly the skulls, of certain classes of criminal have also been collected and often displayed as a warning to the rest of the population of the consequences of murder or treason (Royer, 2003). Body parts from criminals, especially those who had been hanged, had a place in witchcraft, sorcery and alchemy. These bodies would be displayed in marketplaces and other public areas (Royer, 2003). Once removed, the remains might be kept as a warning or they might be taken by the family of the deceased for burial, but generally the bones would be kept and used for a variety of purposes. By the eighteenth century the bodies of those executed in the United Kingdom and many other countries were given to surgeons for dissection (Ward, 2015). This was seen as part of the punishment by many as there was a belief that bodies had to be kept intact for burial so that the whole person could be resurrected (Cunningham, 1997). Human remains were therefore collected for specific purposes, for the science of the day.

1.3   Cabinets of Curiosities

During the sixteenth century modern Western world views began to develop, one of which was a curiosity about the human body. Activities such as dissection had been prohibited by the Christian church for centuries but the Renaissance brought a thirst for new knowledge and a desire to understand the world, particularly the workings of the human body. This began in a furtive and clandestine manner but eventually collections of human bodies and their bones were made by artists, scholars and doctors to aid in their understanding of the human body, and began to be used for teaching (Cunningham, 1997). In art the human skull was often portrayed to remind the viewer of their own mortality. The dissections undertaken at this time began to give a whole new view of the human body and its workings (Momerie *et al.*, 1892). Books showing the viscera of the body and the skeleton were published on the new printing presses. Many of the books are works of art and can still be instructive today.

By the seventeenth and eighteenth centuries, the period known as the Age of Enlightenment, those rich enough to travel began the vast collections that in some cases became the nuclei of many of our present-day museums. They called their collections cabinets of curiosities, and no gentleman felt his collection was complete without at least one or two human skulls. These collections varied in size from actual cabinets or cupboards to room after room of amazing treasures. Many of the collectors had a real interest, one might even say passion, for the material they collected, and even commissioned naturalists, explorers and other travellers to collect on their behalf from the places they visited (Beete Jukes, 1847). The items in these cabinets had often been obtained to the exact specifications of the collector (Impey & Macgregor, 2001). This is where the idea of collection to order has its origin.

It was not just the wealthy who collected; many more ordinary travellers, soldiers, sailors, doctors, especially army or naval, and missionaries collected on their own behalf because of an interest in natural history, a desire for curios from far-away places or because the remains had begun to have a value and it was possible to sell them to rich collectors or to medical schools (Macgillivay, 1852). In addition, for those rich enough to donate there was great kudos to be gained from giving remains to local and later national museums. An examination of the archives, catalogues and index cards of any museum will inevitably show that many of the early acquisitions came from such sources (Clegg, 2009).

1.4   Early Museums

In the eighteenth century many stately homes began to allow visits from the new, more leisured, middle classes to see their collections, for the education and enjoyment of these visitors. They were often inspired in this by their visits, when on the Grand Tour, to both publicly and privately owned collections. Although not open to the general public, it was possible to see these collections at certain times, and this was sometimes how those with treasures of their own made connections with these wealthy individuals.

One of the first national museums in the United Kingdom was the British Museum. This came into existence in 1753 when Sir Hans Sloane, a naturalist, collector and physician, left his collection to the nation for the sum of £20,000 because he wished it to remain intact. The collection consisted of antiquities, books, artefacts, natural history specimens and human remains (Hawkins, 2010). The gift was accepted and an act of parliament set up the British Museum to house the collection. The museum opened to the public in 1759; entry was free, as it is today, and was for all studious and curious persons (Walford, 1878).

The British Museum's collection is a prime example of how collections of human remains accumulated during the eighteenth, nineteenth and twentieth centuries. Almost all museums and institutions whose archives are open to researchers acquired their collections of human remains in similar ways. Some museums were more dependent on one particular route: for example, anatomy museums tended to receive remains primarily from medical schools and doctors and their acquaintances while local museums are often based around archaeological material excavated under a variety of circumstances. The British Museum's donors are used as examples, but also the various different types of donor to the Royal College of Surgeons, London. Interestingly, there were similar drivers for museums in other parts of the world, such as North America, Australia and New Zealand (Bennett, 2004)

1.5   Collectors of Human Remains

The Military

The establishment of public museums in the United Kingdom occurred during the period of expansion of the British Empire. The military were therefore often instrumental in bringing material for British national collections from far-away places, and these almost always included human remains. Both the army and the navy were posted to established parts of the empire and also to survey and establish new routes and trade partners with areas outside the empire (Figure 1.2).

The Navy

During the eighteenth and nineteenth centuries many naval survey voyages were undertaken. These voyages also had a mandate to collect specimens from the places they visited. The ships usually had a naturalist on board for whom detailing and collecting the local flora and fauna was the primary role. He was usually a capable artist who would document not only the local wildlife but also the local inhabitants. The ship's surgeon too was generally interested in natural history and was often an avid collector (Macgillivay, 1852). Ships' officers collected material, as mementoes, as an additional source of revenue or to enhance their status in the eyes of

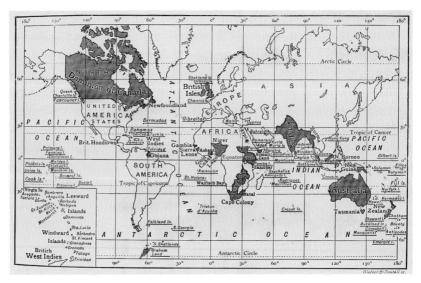

Figure 1.2 Map of the British Empire, *c.* 1800.
Credit: Print Collector/Contributor/Hulton Archive/Getty Images

others by donating to one of the many scientific institutions in the United Kingdom. Even ordinary seamen collected items, including human skulls, either to augment their pay or to take home as curios. This was true in most European countries as well as in the United States and Canada.

The voyages of the *Beagle*, *Rattlesnake*, *Fly* and *Alert* all serve to illustrate the variety of human remains brought back to Britain during this period. The *HMS Fly* not only had a government naturalist but in addition one paid for by the Earl of Derby, a noted collector of the time. The ships' doctors also collected remains; indeed the *Rattlesnake*'s assistant surgeon was one Thomas Huxley, who donated to the Royal College of Surgeons. Many of these ships donated the material collected by their naturalists to national collections, often being given by the Lords of the Admiralty. The vast collection made during the voyage of *HMS Alert* was donated by the Admiralty; only a few of the human remains from the voyage are specifically listed, these being the most interesting examples given to the British Museum (Natural History), now the Natural History Museum (Archives of the NHM London).

The naval officers on the *Rattlesnake*, for example, often traded with the Torres Strait Islanders for human skulls when they visited the islands, situated between Papua New Guinea and Northern Australia, to take on provisions (Macgillivay, 1852). In doing so they were seen as new trading partners in an ancient trade of heads and skulls which stretched from Papua New Guinea right across the strait. Indeed they were often seen as preferred partners as what they offered in exchange was highly prized: metal knives and hatchets, cloth and tobacco. However, there were two differences from the existing partners: the first was that their better weapons made trade more likely to be on their terms than the Islanders' and, second, the skulls were removed from the trading process across the strait.

The Army

When any army unit was posted abroad an army surgeon would be part of the unit. It was usually these men who collected human remains, again mostly skulls. They collected either for themselves, when they saw interesting cases, or they were encouraged to collect for the Royal Army Medical Corps museum, which was building a collection of human skulls for teaching purposes (Williamson, 1857). Many of these skulls eventually found their way into the collections of Oxford University and were transferred to the Natural History Museum during the 1950s and 1960s. On retirement army doctors and surgeons also often gave their collections to the Royal College of Surgeons (Flowers, 1879). These two types of donors gave the remains of a whole range of individuals to museum collections. They included not only local people but also known soldiers and their families, people with strange ailments, traumas and pathologies, which expanded knowledge of illness and injuries much faster than would otherwise have been the case.

Diplomats and Government Officials

Diplomatic postings as governors or ambassadors and as officials working in the colonial service gave ample opportunities for collecting a wide range of material. These items were either brought back to Britain at the end of the overseas service or shipped home at convenient moments, often when moving from one post to another. Many of the human bones that were collected were given to museum collections – often the national collections – which enhanced the donors' view of themselves and sometimes helped in obtaining a further post of their choice. In 1884 the Honourable John Douglas, who had been Premier of Queensland in Australia, donated a Torres Strait mummy to the Natural History Museum (then the British Museum, Natural History) on a trip he made to England that year (Aufderheide, 2002). He was subsequently appointed Government Resident to the Torres Strait. The donation of the mummy showed that he already had contacts within the Torres Strait and to have obtained such an item must be on good terms with influential members of the Torres Strait community and the missionaries who worked there (Figure 1.3), since there was a desire to keep the mummy at the Brisbane Museum. This strengthened his credentials for such a post. It was not of course the donation that did this but the implications of influence and prestige he already held.

Missionaries

Another influential donor who either collected or facilitated the collection of many human remains was W. L. Green. Green was a European merchant who had settled in Hawaii and through his friendship with the Hawaiian monarch and royal family had obtained a post as a government minister (Newbury, 2001). Large numbers of human remains left Hawaii during the time he was in office; they were either directly donated by him to Barnard Davis, who was a large-scale collector of human skulls for his early work in craniometrics, or to visitors such as the Lamberts (Young, 1883) or to the naval officers who came to view the transit of Venus (Airy, 1881). Barnard Davis's collection is discussed later in this chapter.

Diplomats' wives and families also collected human skulls and other bones. Lady Jane Franklin, the wife of Sir John Franklin, the first governor of Tasmania, collected human skulls during her travels with Sir John. In Tasmania she asked George Augustus Robinson, the protector of Aborigines in Tasmania, for a Tasmanian skull when she visited Flinders Island settlement, as did Sir John's secretary (Plomley, 1987). Within a very short period two aboriginal men died and Robinson arranged for the settlement doctor to remove both heads and prepare them to be sent to Hobart for Lady Franklin (Plomley, 1987). One of these skulls was donated by a great nephew of Lady Franklin after the death of her cousin and companion Miss Capstock, who had inherited many of Lady Jane's possessions (Figure 1.4). Investigations during a claim for repatriation narrowed down

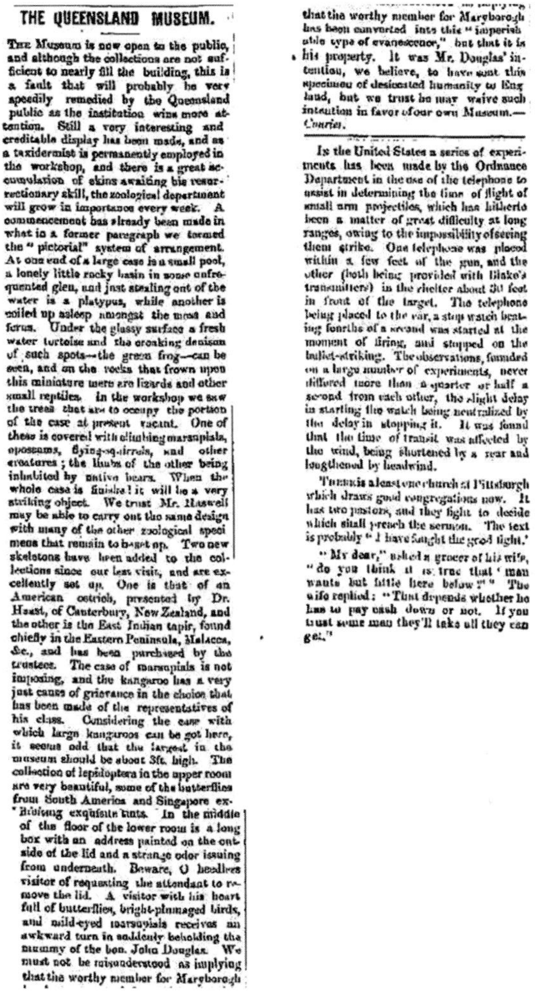

Figure 1.3 TSI mummy referred to as at Brisbane Museum.
THE QUEENSLAND MUSEUM (24 April 1880). *Maryborough Chronicle, Wide Bay and Burnett Advertiser (Qld. 1860–1947)*, p. 4 (SUPPLEMENT TO THE MARYBOROUGH CHRONICLE)

the identity of this skull to one of two individuals, matching them with the account in Robinson's diary.

Missionaries were also influential in the acquisition of human remains from around the world. They were in a privileged position and could often insist that ancient caves or sacred sites were cleared and could obtain

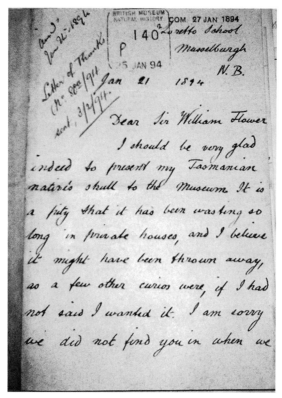

Figure 1.4 Donation letter from Master Trench donating skull to the NHM.
© The Trustees of the Natural History Museum London

ancient remains from such sites or more recent remains from burial grounds no longer used after the local people converted to Christianity (McFarlane, 1888). Many missionaries followed the same pursuits as country parsons in England and were amateur naturalists; this meant they continued collecting many different items, including human remains. These items were often shipped back to the United Kingdom and many were donated or even sold to museums, universities and private collectors. They and other items collected were also a source of revenue for the missionaries, who were often funded a year in arrears.

Doctors and Anatomists

The human remains in museums collected in the past are not limited to those from overseas. Many doctors and anatomists collected remains from

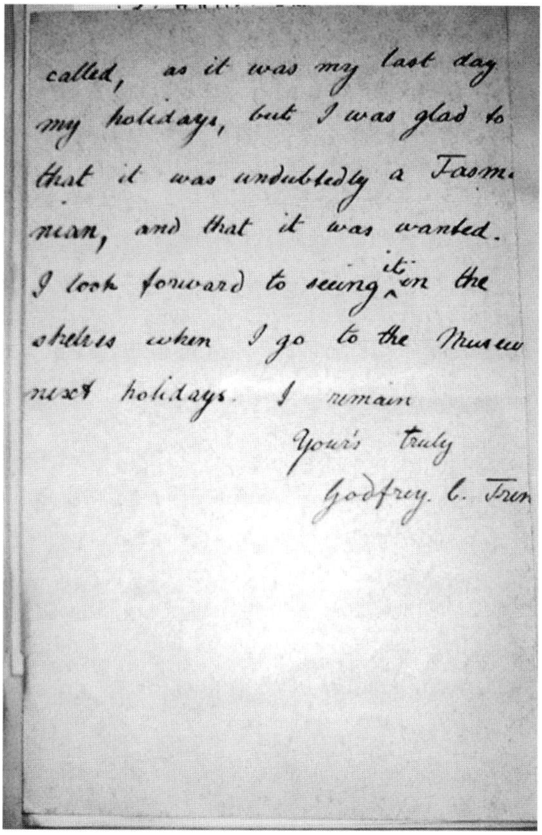

called, as it was my last day
my holidays, but I was glad to
that it was undubtedly a Tasma.
nian, and that it was wanted.
I look forward to seeing it on the
shelves when I go to the Museu
next holidays. I remain
Yours truly
Godfrey. C. Tren

Figure 1.4 (*cont.*)

various sources either through interest or for teaching purposes. They were often held in medical schools or the Royal Colleges such as the Royal College of Surgeons. From the late eighteenth century it was legal to dissect cadavers and the most common source at first was those who had been hanged; indeed dissection was seen as part of the punishment in an age when keeping the body whole was seen as important for resurrection at the last judgement (Ward, 2015). In the nineteenth century it was also common practice for the remains of those who died as paupers, particularly in workhouses, to be sold to anatomy schools for dissection (Fowler & Powers, 2006). Many of the remains were retained and formed the nucleus of university and museum collections. This practice continued well into the twentieth century and was one reason for a reluctance for certain 'hospitals' to be used by the poor. Even in the latter part of the twentieth century many elderly people were reluctant to enter hospitals on these sites, as old memories lingered of the dead disappearing (Courtney, pers. comm.). Even the bodies of those who died in infirmaries were often dissected prior to burial (Dittmar & Mitchell, 2016). Excavations of infirmary burial grounds show that many of the remains originally buried there have evidence of differing degrees of dissection, suggesting at least autopsies being performed (Mitchell *et al.*, 2011).

Bodies were also sold by families, often those living in extreme poverty, who could not afford a burial and whose lives would be improved by the money (Mitchell *et al.*, 2011). This is akin to the situation in countries under colonial rule, when much-needed cash was offered for remains.

Doctors collected remains from interesting cases of all sorts. There was no law preventing them from doing so, and often they retained parts of individuals. This was particularly true of the remains of infants and children (Dittmar & Mitchell, 2016). This tendency continued for many years and eventually culminated in the enquiry into retained tissues at both Alder Hay and Bristol Royal Infirmary which led to changes in practice when human tissue is obtained for medical purposes.

1.6   Early Science

Phrenology

At the end of the eighteenth century Gall hypothesised that our thoughts, behaviour and character were localised in parts of the brain and that these left their mark on the skull (Tyler, 2014). The phrenologist would run their fingers and palms over the head of the person they were examining to determine their exact mix of characteristics. In popular culture this was called having your bumps read, but the phrenologist actually felt for raised areas and hollows on the skull (Figure 1.5). Although we now regard this as pseudo-science it is the basis from which the science of neurology emerged (Tyler, 2014).

By the nineteenth century there were many phrenological societies and practising phrenologists all over the British Isles, France, Germany and the United States (Van Wyhe, 2004). There was an interest in looking at the skulls of individuals of known behaviours such as criminals or idiot savants

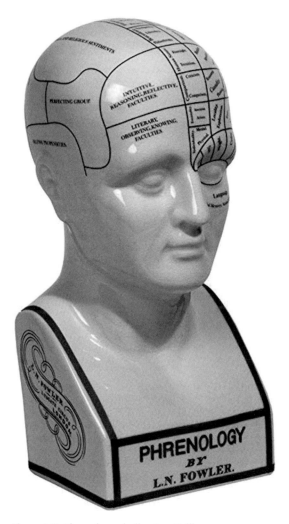

Figure 1.5 Phrenology skull using Gall's map.
Margaret Clegg

and so skulls from a wide range of people were much sort after by phrenologists and these societies (Tyler, 2014). One eminent phrenologist was James DeVille, who amassed an enormous collection of skulls through his contacts all over the world (Browne, 1846). However, by the late 1800s phrenology was largely discredited and phrenologists were no longer consulted.

Craniometrics

Phrenology was largely superseded by craniometry, which used the weight, shape and measurements of the skull to determine such things as the 'race' of an individual (Davis, 1867). One important proponent of this field was Barnard Davis. He not only made his own large collection of skulls but also bought James de Ville's collection. Barnard Davis's collection was vast and encompassed remains from all over the world and from many different time periods. He encouraged those he knew who visited other countries to collect skulls on his behalf (Davis, 1867).

Anatomy

The anatomical understanding of the human body relied on the dissection of human bodies and the examination of skeletal human remains. Dissection became acceptable within the medical profession during the eighteenth century, the Age of Enlightenment. It was not, however, universally acceptable (Mitchell *et al.*, 2011). Many disreputable practices arose which tarnished the growing field of anatomy, from body snatching and grave robbing to failing to inform relatives of deaths in order to be able to sell the bodies to anatomy schools. Despite this, great strides were made in the understanding and treatment of disease and trauma from knowledge gained during such dissections. Although many doctors took a cavalier attitude to human remains they worked to understand the inner functions of the human body on which much of our present-day knowledge and medical understanding has its foundation. The belief accepted within the medical community, which lingers at times even to the present, was that scientific knowledge was all-important and other issues could be set aside to achieve these goals. This has echoes into the arguments about human remains requested for repatriation, in that science is seen as trumping everything, including personal feelings.

1.7   Archaeology

In the nineteenth century there was an interest in past civilisations, among them those within the United Kingdom and Western Europe (Glyn, 1981).

Although to a large extent this was almost a treasure-hunting view of the past, the bones of people from these civilisations were also collected. One area of interest was Egypt, and the mummified remains from tombs and pyramids were brought back to European countries and given to museums or held in private collections. There was a great interest in what the mummy itself looked like and how it was mummified. The Victorians unwrapped many of the mummies they found and skeletonised them in the process (Andrews, 1984). These remains and those still mummified also became part of museum collections.

Within the British Isles excavations were undertaken of barrows and other ancient burial mounds and the remains often put into local museums or, if thought to be important, given by local worthies to national museums. By the late nineteenth and early twentieth centuries archaeological interest had begun to shift toward the locations of either biblical events or those from Greek and Roman literature such as the site of Troy or the hanging gardens of Babylon. Excavations were therefore carried out in the Middle East, Greece and Mesopotamia (Glyn, 1981).

In the Middle East the focus was principally on Bible stories. There were excavations at Jericho, which revealed much about the history of the ancient world. These excavations also contributed many ancient human remains which found their way into national museums including the NHM, the Louvre and, in the United States, to such institutions as the Smithsonian. Many of these institutions initiated their own expeditions to gather artefacts as well as information from archaeological sites all over the world. In Greece and Turkey the locations of the epic poems were sought and the putative sites of Troy, Sparta and Delphi were all excavated (Glyn, 1981). They contributed much to our understanding and also revealed large quantities of human remains. In Mesopotamia, the ancient Sumerian and Babylonian civilisations were examined. One site in Mesopotamia at Ur excavated in the 1930s was not only rich in grave goods but had tombs with multiple burials, allowing death rituals to be reconstructed (Woolley, 1934). This expedition was sponsored jointly by the British Museum and the State University of Pennsylvania. The human remains were given to the Natural History Museum and are still used for research today. Interestingly, one of the archaeologists for this site was Agatha Christie's second husband, Max Mallowell (Christie, 1977). The inspiration for several of her novels, including *Death in Mesopotamia*, have their origin in this and other sites she visited as Mallowell's wife.

Egypt retained its hold and work expanded to Sudan and Nubia. Many natural mummified bodies were discovered, along with large cemetery sites spanning many centuries which allowed changes through time to be examined.

Today most of the human remains that come into museums are from archaeological sites. These are often retrieved as part of rescue archaeology, which is undertaken when building work identifies or unearths human remains or other artefacts, or from planned excavations. The remains may be reburied but generally even when this is the case some analysis is undertaken to ascertain such issues as age and sex and information about burial and mortuary rituals. If reburial does take place then negotiations are undertaken with the relevant authorities and communities, and may be a legal requirement. In England, reburial may be required as part of the licence permitting excavation.

1.8   Issues Surrounding Collecting Human Remains

Many of the remains that are held in museums came into the collections under conditions that we would never countenance today (Palmer, 2002). The remains were often collected without the consent or approval of the local community. Many of the accounts refer to collecting remains when the locals have gone or returning to a cemetery site at night so that no one can complain (e.g. Summers, 1881). It is interesting that so many collectors make reference to this; there can be no doubt that they knew their collecting was not the right thing to do but their belief in themselves and their own desires overrode common decency. In other cases consent was obtained but again we cannot be certain that this was not gained by duress, as there was an imbalance of power particularly when countries were colonised (e.g. Haddon, 1904). This was also true for remains from within the United Kingdom. Here the imbalance was between the doctors and others who worked at the infirmaries and other institutions and the poor who used these institutions. Although the doctors justified the use of these bodies, it was deeply unpopular at the time (Mitchell *et al.*, 2011). There was often a disregard of the law, as can be seen in cases of body snatching from graves both for dissection and for exhibition. Sometimes it was a matter of increasing the offer of money or goods to such an extent that it would have been impossible for the person to resist (e.g. Summers, 1881). Again this was true for the bodies of the dead within countries such as the United Kingdom, as well as overseas remains: the poor would be offered cash for the bodies, often of children. Sometimes, although the trade was legitimate, as in the barter for skulls by the Royal Navy in places such as Torres Strait (Beete Jukes, 1847; Macgillivay, 1852) or the trade in tattooed heads in New Zealand, it was often suspect. The naval officers did not initiate the trade as it was already in existence, particularly in Torres Strait. However, these skulls were often either trophy skulls or forgotten ancestors and in either case the person giving permission or selling the skull may in fact have had no relationship to the person whose remains were sold. This makes issues such as repatriation very fraught as one could argue that there was consent but equally that the person who gave consent had no right to do so.

Even archaeology was not immune to this; many sites were plundered at a time when the country in which the excavation occurred was occupied by another power. Greece is a prime example, being occupied by the Ottoman Empire. The occupying power gave permission for excavations and the removal of remains and objects but it is possible that local people would not have agreed had they been asked (St Clair, 1998).

Today international laws exist to regulate the trade in antiquities including human remains from ancient sites (Vrdoljak, 2008). Many countries have strict regulations regarding what can be done to modern remains and museums now ask that proper paperwork exists before accepting human remains for exhibitions or into their collections. Human remains collected more recently are much more likely to have been collected in an ethical fashion and to be properly documented than those that form the bulk of museum collections.

Many of the issues raised in this chapter will be addressed in subsequent ones. There are ethical, legal and moral questions that need to be examined and explained in regard to the care, exhibition and holding of remains in museums.

Questions

1 What feature found on Neolithic human bones suggests what happened after burial?
A Cut marks
B Weathering
C Burial wrappings
D Mummified skin

2 What inspired the Egyptians to mummify bodies after death?
A Natural mummification
B Finding skeletal remains
C Experimentation on the dead
D Tightly wrapping bodies

3 What body part was retained after death by many cultures worldwide?
A Humerus and radii
B Scapula
C Skull/head
D Ribs

4 What role did cabinets of curiosities play in the development of modern museums?

5 Identify from the following three groups of people likely to donate to museums in the nineteenth century.
A Military
B Doctors
C Diplomats
D Shopkeepers
E Lawyers

6 Give three reasons for the collection of human remains in the past.

7 What use were human remains put to in early scientific research?
Select all those appropriate.

A Phrenology

B Craniometrics

C Finding out about the past through archaeology

D All of the above

One charge often levelled at museums and institutions holding human remains is that the remains sit on dusty shelves and are rarely taken down from those shelves. This may be true in some instances for small, rarely visited museums, but for institutions holding large collections they are an active part of teaching, research, public education and display (Roberts, 2013). The inclusion of human remains in scientific research dates back to the ancient Greeks and Egyptians (Cunningham, 1997). However, it wasn't until the Renaissance that human remains in the form of bones were employed to expand our understanding of the human body. Artists, anatomists and doctors who began dissections of human bodies to understand the inner workings of and potential problems within the body (Cunningham, 1997), all began to turn to skeletal remains to broaden this understanding. During the Enlightenment of the seventeenth and eighteenth centuries the collection and inclusion of human remains for scientific research became more widespread, and indeed many current collections in major museums are based on collections from this time (Mackenzie Wilson, 2002). Human bones and particularly skulls were collected and formed the basis of such diverse fields as phrenology (which although now seen as a pseudoscience has the beginnings of neuroscience at its heart), sources of disease and the documentation of traumas and pathologies (Clegg, 2013a). Interesting cases were sought and their bones collected, many of which became the core of numerous medical museums.

2.1 The Scientific Use of Human Remains in Museum Collections

When remains are claimed for return it is often maintained that they sit on dusty shelves and are rarely used in research. In almost all museums and collections nothing could be further from the truth. Many larger institutions in the United Kingdom, Western Europe and the United States make no distinction between remains that are more popular and less frequently researched remains (see the websites of institutions such as the British Museum, Natural History Museum London, Museum of Natural History in New York, the Museums of the Smithsonian Institute in Washington and the Museum d l'homme in Paris). Indeed, a museum conservator would throw their hands up in horror at such an idea (Clegg & Long, 2015). Most remains in large collections are used extensively by both the museum staff and visiting researchers in a wide variety of research projects (Clegg & Long, 2015).

Early Days

The human remains found in many of the major museums across the world were collected or donated with some idea that they might be of use to the institution for research, although not exactly as we would think of it today (Clegg, 2011). It is often suggested that all institutions had collecting agendas from their inception. This is rarely true; most accepted the human skulls and other bones donated to them on an ad hoc basis and only occasionally had an active collecting policy (Dorland, 2009). However, there are exceptions to this and some museums asked people who were visiting certain places to bring or send remains from the local population to them (Dorland, 2009).

However, it would not be true to say that remains were not collected to 'order'. During the late eighteenth and early nineteenth centuries there was a growing interest in the variation among humans. Initially, two different groups tried to collect large numbers of human remains to further their research: medics and phrenologists. The medics were originally interested in what could be called 'interesting cases': individuals suffering from rare conditions that caused changes to the skull or other parts of the skeleton. However, these doctors soon realised that to understand the changes they found in the abnormal individuals they needed to understand what normal individuals looked like and then compare the differences. One institution that undertook this to a large extent was the British Royal Army Medical Corp (Williamson, 1857). The British Empire was expanding at the time, and army doctors and surgeons travelled with the troops sent all over the world. This was likewise true in countries such as Germany, France, Portugal and Belgium, which also had expanding empires. They collected and sent or brought back vast numbers of skulls.

Phrenology is the science – or pseudoscience, as we now regard it – which saw the skull as providing a map of the brain areas and so enabling an understanding of how the mind and brain were organised. The phrenologists collected huge numbers of skulls from as many different populations as possible to enable them to understand the similarities found in the morphology of the skull, these collections now sit in museums all over Europe and North America (Van Wyhe, 2004). They were also interested in being able to identify the abnormal through this technique, so their collections not only have large numbers of skulls but many are from murderers, the insane, those with congenital abnormalities and both violent and non-violent criminals. These collections are now found in many museums around the world and their diversity contributes to modern research in ways the original donors and collectors could never have imagined.

Some museums also collected ancient human remains, however. This was generally through the funding of expeditions to archaeological sites to search for artefacts. The bones found were collected, though not necessarily as the primary reason for the expedition. These early archaeologists had more in common with Indiana Jones than with their modern counterparts. For the most part they were interested in the treasures from tombs and palaces. For example, the joint British Museum/University of Pennsylvania expedition unearthed amazing artefacts from Mesopotamia which included many sets of human remains (Woolley, 1934), as did excavations of Indian Mounds on behalf of the Smithsonian Institution (Dorland, 2009).

Current Research Using Museum Collections

Human remains are used in a wide variety of research projects, sometimes because they are from a particular population or part of large-scale studies that need to represent as much as possible of the variation found in humans. These projects include human evolution, growth and development studies and human variation either through time or across the world. However, before we look at the type of projects and their results, we need to think about why human remains are important in research and what they can tell us about life in the past, the people themselves and how we can apply this to present-day life. It is important to realise that much of the research undertaken on skeletal remains often has real-world applications (Clegg & Long, 2015). These can range from seeking a better understanding of how children grow and develop, finding the effects of disease on bones and how our activities can shape our skeleton, and looking for disease vectors and parasites in the remains themselves.

When a researcher examines the bones of someone who died long ago they are first looking at that person at the time they died, in essence a snapshot of their life. We can get an indication of how old the person was by looking at their teeth. The reliability varies depending on whether they are an adult or a child, with children's teeth giving a more accurate picture (Figure 2.1). If they died as a child then the number of teeth present or the mix of deciduous and permanent teeth can be used to give a fairly accurate estimate of age within a range of error. This is because our teeth erupt and reach occlusion in the same sequence in all humans; the incisors are the first to emerge, so depending on the particular teeth that are present the child is no younger or older than the normal limits of when these teeth would appear (Smith, 1991).

We can also look at the stage of development of the bones of the skeleton, particularly the long bones and pelvis. Long bones, as with many of our bones, develop from several ossification centres within the cartilage making up children's bones, which gradually increase in size and fuse together to produce the shape of, for example, the femur. How much of this development has occurred can help determine how old someone was when they died (Schuer & Black, 2000).

In adults the wear on permanent molar teeth can give us an approximate age (Brothwell, 1972). These permanent teeth emerge in the same order for all of us so that the first molar, the one nearest to the front of the mandible or maxilla, will erupt and come into occlusion first. It would therefore have more wear than the third molar or wisdom tooth. The amount of wear across these molars allows us to decide if they were very young – when little wear would be seen even on the first molar, or old – when all the molars would be worn down. It is also possible to include the incisors which can in old age be ground down to expose the dentine within the tooth. There are limits to how accurate this can be: for example, a coarse diet can grind the surface of teeth almost flat at a very early age. It is

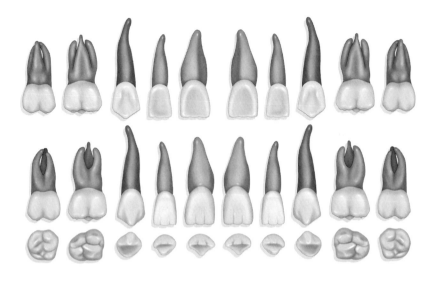

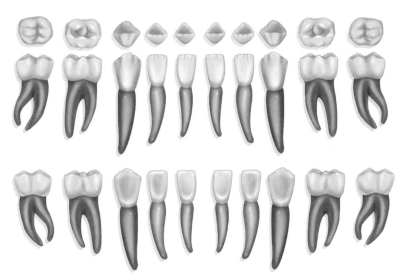

Figure 2.1 Deciduous dentition chart.
Credit: BSIP/Contributor/Universal Images Group/Getty Images

therefore important to use as the reference population for comparison one that has similar dietary and other behaviours which might affect the teeth.

We can determine not just age but general health and what sort of activities someone might have engaged in by looking at the different development of the parts of bones where muscles would attach. We can also look at known differences between men and women, such as the shape of the mandible or pelvis, the presence of a superciliary arch to decide whether the remains are likely to be from a male or female.

If we look a little deeper by using microscopes, X-rays or CT scans and molecular analysis, we can look for information locked inside the bones and teeth, which can expand our knowledge of the person. Microscopic analysis of the teeth can reveal the age the person was when they were weaned. Molecular analysis of the teeth and bones can reveal the person's diet not just when they died, but also during their childhood (Humphrey *et al.*, 2008). This is because teeth are formed when we are very young and do not change at all during our life, so holding the memory of what happened when they were forming. Even the calculus (food debris) between the teeth can provide much information about the diet and disease load of the person during their life. These techniques will be described in a little more detail so that it is easier to understand some of the projects taking place.

Traditional Techniques

Traditional techniques are usually those that involve observations, looking for particular features on the bones or teeth, or that take a series of standard measurements, agreed upon by most researchers and set out in guidance standards such as Buikstra and Ubelaker (1994) or Brickley and Mckinley (2004). We might look at areas of bones where muscles attach, for example. Muscle attachment sites are often clearly visible on long bones. Vigorous or repetitive activity can cause these areas to become more pronounced, and the bones themselves to become thicker and more robust (Pearson & Buikstra, 2009). If the bones of the arm are examined and are found to have strong muscle attachment sites then we would be looking at activities that would require upper body strength – for example if the remains being examined were from the Middle Ages we might suggest that they were an archer, especially if they are male. All medieval men were expected to practise archery from a very early age (Rogers, 2011).

Observations might also tell us if they had suffered any injuries and if so whether they survived them. We can tell if they survived because the old injury would at least show signs of healing (Figure 2.2), although the bone

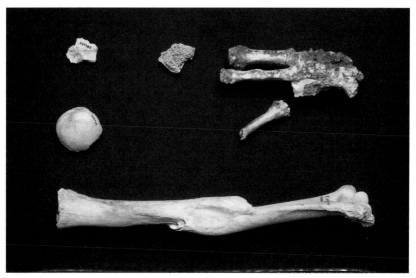

Figure 2.2 Old healed fracture.
Credit: Science & Society Picture Library/Contributor/SSPL/Getty Images

might be pushed out of place because it hadn't been straightened and held in place by a splint (White *et al.*, 2012).

The bones can be measured using standard measurements such as those in Buikstra and Ubelaker (1994) to determine a variety of other information. Long bones can be measured and the height or weight of the individual can be estimated by using an equation. Measurements from the skull can be used in programs such as Fordisk to estimate geographic origin; this is particularly helpful in both forensic and repatriation cases.

More Modern Techniques

In the last twenty or thirty years a whole raft of new techniques have been developed that have expanded our ability to gain new information from these remains. New ways of using X-rays, and developments in genetics and molecular analyses have allowed us to get information previously hidden from researchers. These new techniques, particularly those using imaging, can also give many more people access to the remains than any museum could ever hope to accommodate as visitors.

One exciting technique has been the introduction of CT scans. These were originally developed for medical use and allow us to view the inside of the body as well as the inside of bones and teeth. This has opened up many new avenues to researchers. It is possible to look in more depth at traumas and see the full consequences of these injuries. It is now easy to look at the sinuses of an individual and examine whether or not they suffered inflammation (sinusitis), which can be related to smoky fires or industrial processes (Merrett & Pfeiffer, 2000).

Another major breakthrough has been the development of molecular and chemical techniques such as DNA analysis and isotopes. Molecular and chemical analysis is generally considered to be destructive, which is true, particularly when these techniques were first used. Originally quite a large amount was needed, often a major part of the tooth or bone, and this not only meant that the sample could not be used again but that the bone or tooth that the sample originated from was largely destroyed (see Figure 2.3 for an example of the sample needed).

Figure 2.3 Example of the amount of bone needed for modern molecular and chemical techniques.
Credit: BSIP/UIG/ Contributor/Universal Images Group/Getty Images

Today most techniques require only one gram of material – this would fit onto the nail of your little finger – and the amount needed is getting smaller all the time; it is now possible to use a laser to remove minute quantities with no obvious damage to the tooth.

Advances in technology have made it possible to extract DNA from older and older remains so that the genetics of early populations can be reconstructed. This has allowed us to understand how people in the past migrated across the world, which populations are more closely related and whether in some cases it was people or ideas that travelled (e.g. Szecsenyi-Nagy et al., 2015). Isotopes really do show that we are what we eat. Our bodies are built from the elements we take in as part of our diet and from the water we drink. These minerals are present in different ratios in different types of food and analysing the amount present can provide all sorts of information (Katzenberg, 2007).

Information about diet can tell us what people in the past ate but it can also be used to identify the place a person lived as a child, with samples from the teeth, or as an adult, using samples from bone. This is because there are differences in the isotope ratios between land mammals, marine fish and river fish. For example, in a recent study used to identify which area of South Australia the remains of some Australian Aboriginal people whose exact geographic origin was unknown the ratio of isotopes of terrestrial animals and river fish was crucial in making an identification (Pate et al., 2002). The diet can then be used to confirm a coastal-, river- or land-based location for the person or group of people. Migration patterns can also be distinguished through the use of this technique. A study of a burial site in a place which was a good candidate for initial colonisation by the Maoris was examined. The researchers found that the different groups of burials showed different geographic origins within New Zealand for the individuals, suggesting more mobility and perhaps a return to a site of particular significance after death (Kinaston et al., 2013). The same method using different isotopes can be used to distinguish between different types of plant food from different parts of the world. If you have data from individuals from any area then you can compare your unknown sample with this. Even the water we drink can be used, as it contains the background isotope levels where the person lived as a child or an adult. The results are compared to maps of these background levels and the most likely location determined. These techniques are not only used to aid in archaeological research but are used by forensic scientists to help in identifying the unknown victims of murder, accident or war (Dirkmaat, 2015).

It is possible to laser scan skulls or other bones and build a virtual image of the bone in question (Thompson & Errikson, 2017). This allows far greater access to any collection that has been scanned, as images can be used rather than having to physically go to the museum to collect the data directly from the bones themselves. Scanning also eliminates over-handling of remains, which can cause deterioration of the bones. Scans therefore have the advantage of preserving the remains for the future so that they can be incorporated into research as and when new methods become available. There are, however, issues with this approach as some indigenous communities may have problems with the process and with research access to the scans being granted by the holding institution. There are arguments both for and against undertaking scanning. As stated, scanning does allow access to a wider pool of researchers as scans can be made available digitally without touching the remains themselves. This has advantages in preventing overuse of some parts of collections which may be widely accessed, and it can preserve copies of remains after reburial. For many parts of collections these are not contentious issues and would be a good working practice for such remains (see Figure 2.4 for an example of a scanned image). In the case of remains from indigenous communities this type of data collection should be discussed at an early stage and only undertaken if the community gives agreement. It may be necessary to carry out scans as part of the repatriation process to ensure that all efforts to identify the remains are made. For example, scanning can show injuries or cultural practices not visible to the naked eye and may confirm that an individual underwent processes that are common within a particular culture (Clegg, 2009). If such methods are employed then the community should be given control over the scanned data as part of the repatriation.

2.2   Applications of Research

Research undertaken on human remains in museums and other holding places is, as stated earlier, extremely varied. It can be used to answer a huge

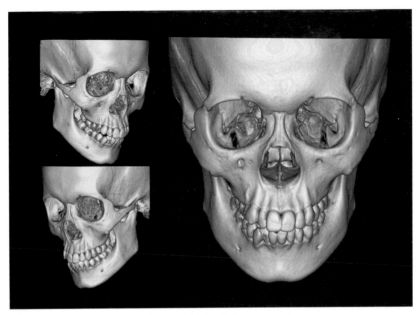

Figure 2.4 Example of a reconstruction of a skull using 3D laser scanning.
Credit: mr.suphachai praserdumrongchai/iStock/Getty Images Plus

range of questions about both past populations and more modern peoples. All human remains have within them the story of the person's life and their interaction with their environment. Such research can also be used to test hypotheses which can then be applied to living populations.

Some research undertaken in the early part of the twenty-first century has shown the incidence of osteoporosis in women from eighteenth- and nineteenth-century England. By examining the density of the long bones in known-aged women from the crypt of Christ Church, Spitalfields, the study showed that the incidence of osteoporosis in these women was at similar levels to those we see today (May, 2000). The researcher had already looked at the bone loss in medieval women and concluded that levels had remained the same for a millennium (May, 2000). This was rather at odds with the accepted idea that there was more bone loss in modern women probably due to their more sedentary lifestyle. This study shows that lifestyle was probably less important than had been expected in determining the rate of loss. Other factors, such as age and hormonal changes, would be more significant.

Surgical teams also use collection of human skeletal remains. They often want to check differences they see when conducting operations. A team recently used the NHM collections to do just this and showed that differences in the pelvis found during surgery were actually part of normal variation rather than, as some thought, due to the presence of arthritis. Other surgical teams have looked extensively at knee joints and used their findings to develop a new keyhole surgical technique for repairing damaged knees.

Collections across the world were instrumental in developing the Out of Africa hypothesis. This has shown that all present-day peoples are closely related and have a single common ancestor (e.g. Stringer, 1978, 1982, 1985). This reinforces the idea that humans are a single species and has done much to undermine the ideas of racial supremacy prevalent from the nineteenth century onwards.

Using fragments of skeletal remains in isotopic analysis has allowed changes in diet in many populations to be charted. This is very important for groups in which diseases such as type 2 diabetes are common. The disease is closely related to obesity, which often occurs in populations once they adopt Western foods and lifestyles. The Pima Indians are a clear example of this: one group of Pima Indians who live in Mexico still practise a more traditional lifestyle, with farming a major activity, but those who live across the border in the United States have a more American lifestyle and the difference is clear to see in the incidence of type 2 diabetes (Schultz et al., 2006). Studying the bones of people around the time that such changes occur can help to determine how much is related to dietary change and how much to activity changes, or if these are related to the poverty often experienced by indigenous communities, whose life chances tend to be lower than the rest of their home population.

Human remains have been used extensively in developing techniques to determine age at death by earlier researchers and continue to be so even today. Two recent new developments have produced a new ageing method and a new dental atlas. The new ageing techniques looked at the wear patterns within teeth and quantified rather than scored the pattern of wear on the teeth. This allowed greater accuracy in the age of the individual which is particularly important in adults (Clements et al., 2008). The other developed a new dental atlas. The atlases in use previously were mostly based on work undertaken in the 1930s. This new atlas was developed using individuals from birth to early adulthood from both living individuals and skeletal collections of known age and sex. This gave broader age ranges for the eruption and occlusion of teeth at each stage of development (AlQahtani *et al.*, 2010).

Sexing children has always been problematic. A recent study using known age and sex children from Spitalfields has shown that the three-dimensional shape of the pelvis can be used to better understand the changes during childhood and so begin to allow sex to be estimated in children (Wilson *et al.*, 2008). The development of adult face shape has also been explored using 3D analysis, and this has implications for determining ethnic origin not only in archaeological samples but in both forensic and repatriation cases too (Strand-Vidorsdottir *et al.*, 2002).

2.3   Caveats when Using Human Remains in Research

There was in the past an assumption among researchers that because human remains were held in a museum there was a right to study them and it did not matter what was done as long as it answered the research question. Equally, many people outside museums thought that remains were of little value once they had been in a museum for any length of time as all the information had been gathered and the remains therefore no longer had any scientific value. Today it is more common to think of the use of human remains as a privilege which needs to be justified so that any researcher should have good scientific reasons to use any remains. There is also engagement with the public showing how human remains are still of value and can make important contributions to human health and well-being. It is becoming more common to have to send a project description to the museum holding the remains so that a variety of issues can be addressed. These include the suitability of the geographic population chosen by the researcher for the research being undertaken. The museum generally checks if this research has already been conducted on this population recently and if so may suggest another population or sample. If the request is to undertake destructive analysis then other issues are also considered, such as the presence of sufficient material of the type requested. For example, if teeth are to be sampled then it is usual to allow this only if an ante mere is present. Whether the remains have been

requested for repatriation or are from a country actively pursuing repatriation of remains is also important. In many institutions it is unusual to
allow research other than that needed to identify the remains if they have
been requested for repatriation. In such cases, or even on indigenous
remains from any country actively making requests even if none is actually
current, the community concerned might be contacted to see how they feel
about the research taking place. Many communities do not want such work
to take place but in some cases – and this is becoming more common –
they may consider granting permission if they feel the project is one they
can support or if it is one they have initiated themselves. Sometimes this
may involve the use of destructive techniques which could ascertain the
affiliation of poorly provenanced remains or to help resolve health issues
within a particular community. It is therefore important to engage with
and if possible work in collaboration with indigenous communities when
undertaking research on ancestral remains from parts of the world that
were colonised in the seventeenth to nineteenth centuries.

A further issue important in deciding access for destructive analysis is
the skill of the researcher and the track record of the lab involved. This is
very important as in all cases the human remains held at an institution is a
finite resource and has to be conserved for the future. It is for example rare
to allow a new technique to be used if it has not first been tested on animal
bones and then more recent human remains. It is also important that if a
researcher wants access as part of a grant-funded project they speak to the
institution staff and get at least in-principle agreement. This ensures that
the museum staff know the researcher wants to come in the future and the
grant agency can be assured that there is agreement for the researcher to
use the collection.

The procedures in place at museums are often seen by researchers as
bureaucratic and as the institution being difficult. However, the demand to
use human remains in research is high and in most museums and other
institutions the number of places available for study is limited. The processes in place allow research that has the greatest chance of success to take
place. In many instances national collections are no longer available to
undergraduates in order to slow deterioration, since, as mentioned earlier,
over-handling causes the deterioration of the bones. At the NHM one only
has to look at the deterioration of the remains from Spitalfields, which has
been more restricted at least over the last ten or fifteen years, to see that

this is the case. Skulls that had been in a single piece now have parts working loose and teeth have come detached from the mandible or maxilla purely through frequency of handling.

If human remains in museums are to be available to future researchers then such restrictions are necessary. However, the digitisation of remains will improve access as basic routine research or initial training can take place using the digitised version with newer or novel research using the actual bones when necessary. In some cases this will seem as though the restrictions are greater but access to a version of the remains will be widely available.

Questions

1 Which of the following are the types of research undertaken on human remains?
A Dental development
B Sex differences
C Effects of trauma
D All of the above

2 Name two traditional techniques for studying human remains.
A Measurements
B Observations
C Photography
D X-rays

3 How do scientific methods help in repatriation?

4 What might be problematic for indigenous groups about scientific research on ancestral remains? Choose all those appropriate.
A They haven't given consent
B May upset the ancestors
C Poor information
D Work not explained to them
E All of the above

5 What needs to be considered before permission is given to access remains for research including destructive testing?

A Does the researcher have relevant experience?

B Have the remains been used recently in similar research?

C How important are the remains?

D Are they likely to be repatriated?

E All of the above

6 Give two reasons why scanning remains is important.

A Preserve collection for the future

B Allow access without touching the physical remains

C Great fun to do

D Always use the latest methods

3 The Legal Aspects of Human Remains

Most countries have laws governing human remains. These range from treatment of the body after death through use of organs from the dead, the excavation of remains from cemeteries and other situations. There are sometimes specific laws for archaeological human remains but more generally these are covered under any laws relating to national or cultural heritage (Márquez-Grant & Fibiger, 2011). More recently consideration has also been given in law to the return of human remains held in museum and other collections to their country of origin. This has been more widely contested than any of the other laws. It is a case where the law and ethics come into conflict, see Chapter 4 for a fuller discussion.

When people in a wide variety of countries are asked about how remains should be treated the terms dignity and respect are the most widely used. In most countries people are concerned that the dead, both recent and more ancient, are treated well immediately after death and subsequently, should their remains be uncovered at a later stage (Giesen & White, 2013). What this actually means varies from region to region and sometimes within the same country, particularly in countries with a federal state. Even the definition of human remains may differ from state to state. Although we all agree that human remains are the whole or parts of once living people from our own species Homo sapiens (Giesen & White, 2013), some countries exclude fossilised hominids, others exclude hair and nails, while yet others consider everything, including soft tissue and slides containing microscopic fragments, as remains. The issue is not a simple one although it appears on the surface to be so. It would not matter so much that these differences exist if knowledge regarding the law in this area was clearly understood. Unfortunately many members of the public and even those who work for museums and government departments are not always clear as to the law in their own country. To quote a colleague of mine who lectures in this area, 'read the laws, do not rely on others to interpret for you' (Giesen, pers. comm.[1]).

3.1   Historic Perspectives

Laws governing the treatment of the dead and the exhumation or disinterment of skeletal remains are among the earliest regarding the treatment of the body after death. The earliest reference is in the epic of Gilgamesh (George, 1999) which shows an expectation that even the bodies of fallen enemies should be given appropriate death rituals so that their ghosts would not cause harm. The tablets setting out Hammurabi's code in ancient Mesopotamia shows that those sentenced to capital punishment would not be given proper burial rites after their death and so were exiled from the netherworld thus putting their own family at risk from their ghost. Furthermore this denial of burial rites was extended to enemy soldiers during war; their bodies were not buried but burned in order to totally destroy them and prevent their onward journey into the next world, seen as an additional victory over the enemy. This idea of the connection between the spirit and the body is common throughout the ancient world. The Egyptians believed that the body and spirit were separate but that the body needed to be preserved to ensure the ability to live forever in the next world (Clarysse, 2011). These rites are set down in some of the earliest laws in Egypt. Even today many different cultures still have this tie between the bodies and spirits of the dead.

One interesting aspect is that any legislation ensured that the body was disposed of in a manner which would not cause a public health issue. Even the total destruction of the bodies of criminals and enemy soldiers ensured this.

In the Roman period, during the republic and early empire, there was strict legislation regarding the disposal of the dead. This legislation dealt with remains in a hygienic way and in accordance with Roman beliefs (Relief & Cilliers, 2005). All burials and cremations except those for very small babies had to take place outside the city or settlement. This led to the establishment of formal cemeteries. Even at this time executed criminals

[1] Lecture at Royal College of Surgeons 2013.

were denied burials and those crucified were often allowed to rot away on their crosses. Desecration of graves was an offence punishable by death. Cemeteries were protected as sacred spaces but given their lonely setting they became dangerous not only because of the belief that they could be haunted but because thieves, beggars and the destitute used them (Toynbee, 1996).

In later times, with the advent of Christianity, laws surrounding disposal of the dead came under the aegis of the church as part of canon law (Daniell, 1997). The pope had ultimate responsibility and all monarchs owed duty to him as God's representative. Burials followed quickly after death, as they did in the Jewish religion from which the early laws were drawn. Soon after the permanent adoption of Christianity in Europe burial sites changed and areas around the church began to be used. Canon law then only sanctioned burial in these places; only suicides and those who suffered capital punishment were buried in unconsecrated ground (Daniell, 1997). Disturbing the dead was seen as unacceptable and to be avoided.

3.2   The Current Legal Approach Worldwide

In ethical terms we could divide the dead into four categories. This is set out in more detail in Chapter 4:

- The newly dead
- The recently dead
- The long dead
- The ancient dead

Legally the first two categories are generally well protected with more limited legislation for the final two categories, usually termed archaeological remains (Clegg & Long, 2015).

In most countries there are a variety of laws dealing with the disposal, treatment and exhumation of the dead. There is a wide variation between countries as to how these are dealt with, but most laws and statutes currently in place provide for the hygienic disposal of the dead and, if burial is the normal custom, provide a framework though which remains can be exhumed and the circumstances under which this can happen.

There are also generally laws to place responsibility for the discovery of human remains in unexpected places (Márquez-Grant & Fibiger, 2011). In almost all cases these remains are treated as forensic cases until proved otherwise. The exact method used to inform and the appropriate authority to contact does vary but there is usually a legal requirement to do so. The disposition of the remains should they prove not to be recent is probably the most variable. In some countries the remains are placed in museums, while in others they are either buried or cremated depending on local custom and tradition. The majority of countries worldwide treat ancient or archaeological human remains as part of the cultural or heritage property of the country. Some countries, particularly those with a great reverence for ancestors, have different rules and often specific places for the interment of such skeletal remains (Márquez-Grant & Fibiger, 2011).

The focus of this chapter will be European countries, the United States, Canada, Australia and New Zealand. However, other countries such as China, South Africa and South America will be referred to when there are specific laws that impact on human remains, particularly for repatriation or archaeological excavation. Human remains will be discussed in terms of the two categories that are generally given legal protection. Recent deaths and archaeological remains are usually treated differently and there is generally a specific cut-off date to distinguish between the two types. Unfortunately, this date is different in many countries and can lead to confusion when working with human remains around the world. Márquez-Grant and Fibiger's (2011) edited volume gives a good introduction to the laws relating to human remains across the world. The chapters are written by people working in those regions and as such give local knowledge of the law. If more detailed information is required then their book is a good starting point. However, the law does change over time and it is important to check government websites and recent publications from the geographic location of interest; some of these websites are listed below in this volume's reference section. It is also important to remember that generally the law from one country is not valid in another. For example, the United States has the Native American Grave Protection and Repatriation Act (NAGPRA) but this only applies within the United States and not in other countries holding Native American remains.

The Newly and Recently Dead

There is wide variation in how countries deal with issues relating to the newly and recently dead. Most Western European countries have laws similar to those of the United Kingdom. The United Kingdom will therefore be used as an example of the types of law in place.

In England and Wales there have been laws in place for the burial and treatment of the dead since before the Middle Ages. During the nineteenth century a series of laws including the Anatomy Act (1832) and the Burial Act 1857 came in to force. The Anatomy Act was amended many times during both the nineteenth and twentieth centuries until it was superseded by the Human Tissue Act in 2004. The Burial Act 1857 is still in force and covers all exhumations including of archaeological remains, although it has been revised and amended many times to cover changing burial practices such as cremation. This latter is different from many other European countries where specific laws pertain to archaeological remains.

The Human Tissue Act (2004) brought together a number of different pieces of legislation and also addressed newer issues that had not previously been fully regulated. The Act rules on all aspects of human remains including transplants, DNA analysis and display of bodies and skeletal remains. It covers human remains under 100 years old held in museums and other institutions and sets up a proper licensing system for all areas of work which are undertaken on any type of human remains. For those who hold human remains in their collections it has several impacts. All human remains less than 100 years old (this is a rolling date from the present) have to be held under a licence for either research or public display (Human Tissue Act, 2004). Most collections will need a licence for public display. A licence is required not only if remains are actually on display but if they may be made available to the public, who under the Act are any persons not part of the holding institution. For example, a licence would not be needed by a university that only used remains for teaching purposes, but if these remains might be used on open days or as part of outreach then a licence would be needed. The licence also covers any research that might be conducted on the remains. All museums that hold remains less than 100 years old need to apply for a public display licence. The 100-year time scale was chosen because living people are more likely to have a direct and close genealogical relationship with the remains held by the museum. The

Act also allowed the nine national museums[2] to deaccession remains that are less than 1,000 years old, enabling these museums to return remains to their country of origin or to genealogical descendants. In the case of repatriation a longer time period was chosen as this was thought to be an appropriate time span for demonstrating a close and continuous geographic, religious, spiritual and cultural link to the remains. The Department of Media, Culture and Sport's guidance on human remains gives further information regarding these time scales.

The Burial Act 1857 still remains in force and under its provisions a licence, originally from the Home Office but now from the Ministry of Justice, is required before human remains in cemeteries or churchyards are disturbed. A licence is also needed if it seems likely that remains will be uncovered as part of an excavation outside these areas. The licence can be applied for retrospectively if remains are uncovered unexpectedly. As part of the application process the final disposition of the remains must be stated; however, this can be modified at a later stage should circumstances change. If remains are in a Church of England churchyard then a faculty to disinter must also be applied for from the local diocese.

All human remains that are discovered in an unexpected setting have to be reported to the police. The remains are examined by a pathologist or a forensic anthropologist depending on their condition. This is to ascertain if they are likely to be the subject of a criminal investigation. If the remains are shown to be more than fifty years old they are unlikely to be investigated by the police. Depending on the age and the context remains will either be cremated or become part of a museum collection.

There are several areas common to most countries. The first is that all human remains found in unexpected places must be reported to the police. They are usually then treated as forensic cases and an investigation mounted to determine if they are dead through criminal activity or to identify them as a missing person. The time period for considering remains as recent varies greatly and may be anything from fifty years to a hundred years depending on the country. If the remains are determined to be archaeological then usually all investigations cease, although when specific

---

[2] British Museum, Natural History Museum London, Museum of London, Science Museum, Victoria and Albert Museum, Museums of Liverpool, National Maritime Museum, The Royal Armouries and the Imperial War Museum.

legislation is in place for any category of remains, as in the United States or certain European countries, then these continue until all information is collated. These categories will be discussed in the next section.

The second is that if the recently dead are to be exhumed then a licence must be obtained from the relevant authorities. In the United Kingdom this is the Ministry of Justice; in the United States it is the body nominated by the state in which the exhumation is to take place, generally through a court order (Márquez-Grant & Fibiger, 2011). The responsibility for safe disposal is also common throughout most of the world; although the practices may vary there is generally a legal obligation for such disposal and it must use the local mortuary customs.

The Archaeological Dead

Legally this is a huge category and there are sometimes different treatments for remains depending on specific circumstances within a country. This section will start by looking at the more general type of laws that apply to archaeological human remains.

The common legal requirement in most countries is that if you wish to excavate human remains then you must obtain a licence, although even this isn't standard and in some countries human remains have less legal protection than historic artefacts. That said, most European and North American countries as well as Australia and New Zealand will only allow excavation with a licence or permit from the relevant government department or institution mandated by the government to issue them (Márquez-Grant & Fibiger, 2011). More recently in New Zealand excavations of any Maori dead has to have the permission of the local Maori Elders (Buckley & Petchey, 2018). In certain countries such as those in Eastern Europe or some in South America excavations can only take place with the involvement of a designated institution within the country, often the National Museum or a major university (Márquez-Grant & Fibiger, 2011).

In many countries there is no specific legislation setting out how archaeological human remains should be dealt with and they are usually covered by laws relating to cultural or national heritage (Márquez-Grant & Fibiger, 2011). In the United Kingdom and in some other countries there is a legal requirement that when major development occurs the developer must have an archaeologist on site with a watching brief to ensure that any archaeological artefacts including human remains are fully documented and exposed in an appropriate manner (Chartered Institute for Archaeologists, 2015). Furthermore, the cost of such work has to be met by the developer.

3.3   Special Cases

Repatriation

As Chapter 1 has shown, human remains have been collected from a large number of places and most countries have human remains from all around the world. These remains were often collected in circumstances that today we would find not only unethical but repugnant (Clegg, 2013a). Some of the remains currently in all our museums fall into this group. To address this issue and to allow museums to return remains should they be requested many countries now have laws that either make return mandatory or allow institutions previously prohibited by law from returning to do so (e.g. Human Tissue Act, 2004; Native American Graves Protection and Repatriation Act, 1990). In general the mandatory returns are to allow remains to be returned within a country to the indigenous peoples from that country. In countries with minority indigenous populations there is rarely legislation to return remains to overseas indigenous communities, while the laws that allow repatriation tend to be in countries which would usually only make international repatriations. In England and Wales this is covered by the Human Tissue Act 2004, which gave permission for the English National Museums to deaccession human remains less than 1,000 years old from their collections. Previously, English National Museums could only deaccession any item from their collections under specific conditions such as damage beyond repair or duplication, neither of which was applicable to human remains. In France, museums also could not deaccession but recently an exception has been made for Maori remains and it is likely that Australian Aboriginal remains will soon be granted the same exemption.

In the United States two laws have been passed which grant the right of return of Native American remains to First Nations. The Native American Graves Protection and Repatriation Act (NAGPRA, 1990) gave the right of return across the United States to human remains that could be shown to be affiliated to a First Nation. It required all museums to produce listings of the remains they held and to engage with First Nation groups over how remains would be returned. The National Museum of the American Indian Act (NMAIA, 1989) set up a separate museum at the Smithsonian Institute and also provided funding for the Smithsonian Museums to audit their human remains holdings. They were to engage with First Nations to ensure the return of affiliated human remains. In both cases funding is provided by these Acts of Congress. In the first case the monies are mostly to allow visits by First Nations representatives to the museums and also to pay for the transportation of the remains on return. In the second case the NMNIA provided funding not only for the new museum and as in the NAGPRA for First Nations to engage but also to fund the documentation of the very large volume of Native American human remains held at the Smithsonian Museums, in excess of 20,000.

There is a further piece of legislation, this time in international law, which may be relevant to human remains. The Hague Convention on cultural property in the event of armed conflict was brought about after devastating cultural destruction that took place during World War II to safeguard cultural property during conflicts. States undertake to protect not only their own cultural property but that of other states. They agree not to target sites of cultural interest and to have specific units in their military to safeguard such property. This also applies to armies of occupation. All cultural property removed from a country must be returned after the conflict and criminal proceedings will be initiated if this does not happen. The convention was proposed in 1954 and enacted in 1956. It has two protocols. The original one which came into force at the same time as the convention requires states to safeguard cultural sites and artefacts. A second protocol was proposed in 1999 and enacted in 2004; this gave states the ability to list sites with enhanced protection, making them immune from both attack and from use as military bases by the home state.

Cultural artefacts and other property have thus been protected since 1956. Many states have ratified one or both protocols. The most recent was the United Kingdom in 2017. Many states regard human remains as cultural property, particularly those older than approximately 100 years. As far as could be found there have been no cases where the Hague Convention has been used to return remains, but there could be grounds for its use. Many colonial powers would under the terms of the convention have been armies of occupation, and much earlier than the date of the convention human remains have been moved from one country to another through transfers and purchases. In the case of remains having been brought to a colonising country, particularly if it had been occupying the home country in the past, then it might be possible to use the convention. Some museums have at times refused to return remains such as Mokomokai (New Maori tattooed heads) because they were cultural objects rather than human remains (e.g. British Museum). Although not directly applicable, the highlighting of a signatory of the convention not returning such objects might be embarrassing and strengthen the case being argued by the claimant community.

War Dead

In many countries there have been recent or fairly recent conflicts ranging from world war battles to civil war. Countries, particularly in Europe, have passed specific laws relating to this class of human remains. In France, Belgium and Germany there are laws to both protect the cemeteries in which the dead of the First and Second World Wars are buried. Details of the individual legislation for each European country can be found in Peaslee (1974). Furthermore, any human remains found in areas of these countries associated with battles in the two world wars are subject to analysis to determine if they are war dead and if so are buried with military honours. The law makes it an offence to remove remains without permission and without notifying the local authorities.

In other parts of Europe where recent conflicts and civil wars have occurred, such as Kosovo, Serbia, Croatia and Bosnia, countries cooperate with international bodies after the conflict has ceased to find those killed during the war. This has several aims: to find those killed, especially civilians, and to return their bodies or remains to their families; to look for evidence of war crimes; and to bring those responsible to justice. It is organised through the International Commission for Missing Persons (ICMP, www.icmp.int). Many teams of forensic anthropologists have given their time to aid in this work and have found the remains of many people but the work continues.

In the United States and several other countries the military have as part of their mandate to bring home all soldiers who die in foreign wars, and they may set up special projects for specific battle sites. The United States, for example, has a special unit in Hawaii, the Defence POW/MIA

Accounting Agency at Joint Base Pearl Harbor-Hickamto, to undertake this work and it is currently examining remains found in a number of countries including Vietnam, Iraq and Afghanistan.

3.4   Conclusions

In legal terms several classes of human remains have been the subject of legislation to protect them. Legislation for the newly and recently dead provides for hygienic disposal and to minimise disturbance after burial takes place. There are also international conventions to find war dead and if crimes were committed during the conflict then to find and prosecute the perpetrators. The public display of the recent dead may also require a licence in some countries. The archaeological dead often have fewer protections but in many countries strict rules have to be followed before exhumations may take place. Human remains found unexpectedly are almost universally treated as forensic cases until proved otherwise. War dead, regardless of age, are treated as a separate class of remains particularly in countries which have been sites of conflicts in the past 100 years. When working with human remains, no matter where in the world, it is essential to familiarise oneself with the relevant law before undertaking any excavations, research or public display.

Questions

1 Which of the following are referred to by most people when discussing human remains?
   A Dusty museum shelves
   B Dignity and respect
   C Consent
   D Scientific research
   E All of the above

2 Which was the first civilisation to have written rules governing disposal of the dead?
   A Egyptians
   B Babylonians

C Romans

D Celts

3 Which two categories of the dead have the most legal protection in most countries?

A Ancient dead

B Recently dead

C Newly dead

D Long dead

4 What is the cut-off time period for human remains in collections to be covered by the United Kingdom's Human Tissue Act after which a licence is no longer required?

A 1,000 years

B 100 years

C 50 years

D 5,000 years

5 What did the Human Tissue Act allow English national museums to do?

A Collect human remains

B Return remains to country of origin

C De-accession human remains

D Rebury all human remains in their collections

6 What is the most common legal requirement to be fulfilled before excavating human remains?

A Have permission of the landowner

B Excavate in conjunction with an institution in the home country

C Obtain a licence to excavate

D Most countries have no legal requirements

7 What is the name of the first United States law regulating Native American human remains?

A Native American Grave Protection and Repatriation Act

B National Museum of the American Indian Act

    C Human Tissue Act

    D Cultural Property Act

8 What international organisation coordinates excavations of war dead in countries such as Serbia?

    A The Council for Refugees

    B The International Commission for Missing Persons

    C Interpol

    D The International Court of Justice

9 What is the name of the US agency that is mandated to bring home war dead?

    A The Department of Defense

    B Prisoners of War and Missing in Action Accounting Agency

    C Homeland Security

    D The Senate Committee for Defense

10 What is legally most important if you are responsible for human remains?

    A Having a good technical knowledge

    B Having an understanding of the law relating to human remains

    C Talking to indigenous communities

    D Storing remains safely

4   Ethical Considerations for Human Remains

There has been a growing interest in and discussions of ethical issues surrounding the collection, storage and use of human remains in scientific research in recent years. Many professional bodies have drawn up ethical statements and codes of practice to help to guide their members in their approach to human remains (e.g. British Association of Biological Anthropology and Osteoarchaeology (BABAO), American Association of Physical Anthropology (AAPA)). However, despite the growth of ethical statements there needs to be a fundamental understanding of what is meant by ethics and taking an ethical approach. To do this we need to look at what considerations need to be given when thinking about such issues.

4.1   What Do We Mean by Ethics?

Ethics are the standards of right and wrong that proscribe certain behaviours. This is framed within the terms of rights, fairness, obligations to others, including society, and benefits to society (Blackburn, 2001). Ethics is not about what is legal, what society accepts, how we feel, or even necessarily about religion. An ethical stance and its application is really about human rights and dignity. Behaviours and laws may be accepted but if unjust or compromising human dignity or rights then they are unethical.

Ethical approaches can be taken in many different fields of life and work. Today there is much discussion regarding being ethical but as this is not an area usually taught outside a philosophy class it can be difficult for people to truly understand what this means. Two issues stand out here. The first is natural justice. If human remains have been removed from burial grounds, for example, and the individuals' descendants want them returned then it would be just to do so even if the remains can be of great benefit scientifically or medically (Scarre, 2009). The second is the issue of consent. This is today the foundation of many pieces of legislation and codes of practice which require ethical behaviour. In most cases the remains being requested for repatriation had no consent obtained from either the person or their relatives for the remains to be taken and placed in a museum. Indeed, as stated in Chapter 5, many of the named individuals, particularly from indigenous or other disadvantaged groups held in collections specifically requested not to be put in a museum. Consent is often overlooked in many spheres, especially in the past when 'doctor knows best' was the order of the day (Mitchell *et al.*, 2011). It is at the heart of some human remains legislation, for example the English Human Tissue Act, which in the section on both public display and donation for medical science (Part 1, section 3), excluding organ donation, needs the consent of the person who will be displayed or used in science. In our large and complex societies we need sometimes to be explicit in defining who can and can't give permission and this is what such legislation tries to do. It is also justified to ask if the dead can give consent but in many medical situations close relatives can make such decisions and this may be one way of providing consent for more modern collections and regularising legacy collections.

In some respects, though, humans are actually ethical beings; not in that they always behave well but in that they constantly compare admire and justify actions (Blackburn, 2001). Even children have an instinctive feel for when things are not 'fair'. They will naturally try to be fair, for example when dividing sweets and knowing that someone has more or less than them. Our love of gossip about friends, enemies and famous people also shows this, as do the dilemmas often shown in soap operas: when one character knows that another is cheating on a third do they tell and betray one friend or not tell out of loyalty to another.

It is often easier to understand if we look at some situations and decide whether the behaviour is ethical. As we have discussed in Chapter 3, all cultures have burial rituals and one of the punishments for the loser in a battle is to be denied burial. As long ago as the ancient Greeks Sophocles' play *Antigone* shows the conflict for the heroine: does she obey the king who has forbade burial or does she bury her brother who is among the dead? The latter wins. The ancient Greeks understood, as do we (Blackburn, 2001), that Antigone's sense of honour demanded burial of her brother no matter what the law. Looking at this in a more general way, several scenarios come to mind. A very old one is a variant of this: in a hospital there are five people who will die if not given a transplant. A man with no relatives comes to the hospital, if he is killed then no one will miss him and five people's lives will be saved. This very obviously would be unethical but other arguments have been used at different times to justify similar actions.

In terms of repatriation, if remains have, as was the case for Truginini, been obtained despite the known objections of the person during their life, then this is unethical. In many cases when you read the accounts from the time, when raiding graveyards and collecting skeletal remains it is obvious that the people collecting knew that their behaviour was unacceptable: they speak of waiting until dark or for the relatives to leave (Clegg, 2013a). Other cases seem not so clear-cut. For example, the British Navy bought skulls from islanders in the Torres Strait (Beete Jukes, 1847; Macgillivay, 1852; Haddon, 1904). This was at the time a well-established trade and the Navy became a new trading partner. However, many of the skulls were trophies taken from enemies from other islands who certainly would not have given consent. To make this more obvious, we can substitute the purchase of people as slaves from African slave traders. This was a well-established trade in Africa and the Europeans became new trading partners (Rawley & Behrendt, 1981). This makes it obvious that it is a matter of consent but the purchase argument has been used to justify retaining remains that had been purchased from the wider indigenous communities within a country.

Several other interesting case studies are presented by Schrag (1997, 2006a, 2006b) in which he looks at scenarios relating to human remains either held in museums or recently discovered during construction work. The scenarios are ones likely to arise in situations when there is legislation in place and some would occur whether there was legislation in place or not. All of the cases are discussed in terms of NAGPRA and make interesting reading. There are also commentaries on the ethical stance that should be adopted.

4.2   Are All Human Remains the Same?

One issue that needs to be considered is whether all human remains can be treated in the same way. Is it possible to apply the same ethical consider-ations to all human remains no matter what their age or source? There are many ways in which one might separate human remains into different classes or categories. One often used is the age of remains. This has, for example, been used in the Human Tissue Act (2004) in the United Kingdom to allow certain human remains to be de-accessioned from national collections and was also used when deciding the fate of Kennewick man in the United States (Rasmussen *et al.*, 2015). If we follow this convention then four categories of human remains based on time period can be considered. These are:

- The newly dead – deaths among relatives of living people.
- The recently dead – those whose identities we may know and of whom we may have intergenerational knowledge.
- The long dead – deaths from a time when we are less likely to have any knowledge of the individual's personal identity.
- The ancient dead: from civilisations and societies that no longer exist and are far removed from present-day societies.

In most countries different rules apply for the treatment of remains from each of these groups. In public perception these categories are also considered differently. The outcry when children's organs were found in UK hospitals is very different from the expectation by the same public to see human remains from ancient times in museums when they visit them (Historic England, 2009). These differences are even enshrined in law, with legislation such as the 2004 Human Tissue Act in the United Kingdom which regulates everything from organ donation to public display of the remains of the newly dead. The primary consideration again is one of consent. The recently dead have long had a degree of protection in law through such legislation as the Burial Act 1857. However, the long and the ancient dead do not have any similar protections. The current legislation was looked at in detail in Chapter 3. The legislation that is enacted in many countries does seem to have at its core a degree of ethical consideration. However, it was not always so; nor can we rely on this to be the case in the future or in all countries. From the seventeenth century onwards in England it was legal for the bodies of executed criminals to be given to the surgeons for dissection, this was at a time when Christian belief held that to be resurrected the body had to be kept intact (Hurren, 2016). In effect the punishment for the crime continued after death. There was often fierce resistance to this, with fights between the surgeons' servants and the family and friends of the executed person (Cunningham, 1997). When this law was repealed, a source of bodies was still required for teaching and researching anatomy. A new law came into force in the early nineteenth century which allowed the authorities running workhouses, sanitaria and mental institutions to sell the bodies of inmates not claimed by their families without making it mandatory to notify the inmate's family of their death (Hurren, 2012). A lucrative source of revenue was thus available and the practice continued into the 1930s in the United Kingdom. It is also easy to see times when for a variety of reasons treatment of the recently dead might not comply with ethical standards although it may be completely legal. It has been the case in many countries that the dead, both recent and long dead, are treated differently depending on the class or group in society. The case above is an example but there are, especially within colonial countries, examples of major differences between how the settlers' dead are treated and how the indigenous population is treated. This has continued in some countries into modern times. In the United States the majority of human remains in museums are Native American and have often been obtained from ancient and not so ancient burial grounds (Fine-Dare, 2002). This has led to a perception that only Native American remains are used by scientists in museums. In the United States this was largely true, as it is within other European settled countries such as Australia. When groups ask for remains held in countries other than their own to be returned they bring this perception with them. However, in most European countries the predominant category of remains is European. It is therefore often a surprise to indigenous representatives visiting museums in the United Kingdom and Western Europe, when they ask about which remains are most used, to find that the highest number of research visits are to European remains, generally those from the local country. For example, the two most researched collections in the Natural History Museum, London are those from Christ Church, Spitalfields in East London and Romano-British remains from Poundbury in Dorset, both United Kingdom locations.

There have been some investigations in countries settled by Europeans which have large indigenous populations about the view of other remains in museums. In 2007, Te Papa Museum in New Zealand had a large exhibition on Egypt, which included human remains in the form of mummies. The exhibition was well received but a comment on the museum's blog pages set off a discussion in New Zealand about showing other people's ancestors when you were asking for the return of yours. This also started a long discussion with Maori Elders about the exhibition (New Zealand Herald, 2006). Interestingly, many people came to the view that because these people were from an ancient civilisation and their nearest descendants didn't want them returned but were happy for them to be exhibited (some remains had been loaned by the Egyptian Museum in Cairo) that this was permissible. So even in countries with a long history of asking for remains to be returned, the very ancient dead, from a different culture, may sometimes be considered a different class of remains.

I have set out one possible method of considering human remains and it is the one often used by those who work with human remains. However, in former colonial countries human remains may be treated differently depending on whether they are from the indigenous or colonising community. In the United States, for example, it is rare today to see Native American human remains displayed. This leads to the position exemplified in a recent Smithsonian exhibition when a European and an African American skull were displayed but the Native American was obviously a cast. This was of course to address the sensitivities of Native American nations but left a glaring contrast which drew attention to this disparity of treatment.

By acting ethically even when this means that remains must be returned, researchers can then more easily justify the ways in which they use human remains. It is also important to talk to descendants of people whose remains are in our museum collections from both at home and abroad to show how the scientific study of human remains can help to address some of the problems suffered around the world through illness, disease and trauma. This may help the claimant communities understand why it is that the scientists involved value the remains. This may not change minds but does show that the researchers involved are not doing it out of disrespect. That said, research should not be undertaken without regard to others. It is preferable to engage with people to explain what we do and why. It is also important to show that human remains are treated ethically.

4.3   The Ethics of Using Human Remains in Research

When repatriation was first proposed the usual response from an institution or academic who used remains in their research was that the use of the remains was for the greater good. It was proposed that science trumped the feelings and rights of the descendants of the people whose remains were held in the museum. This, as pointed out earlier, is not an ethical stance. It suggests that scientific research, no matter of what time, is more important than the feelings of living people and that scientists are somehow better than non-scientists. One can think of many examples of this justification from grave robbing to experiments using captives, prisoners of war or those in concentration camps.

We, as curators and researchers, now for the most part acknowledge that it is a privilege not a right to access and research human remains (BABAO, 2016). In the early days of repatriation the return of remains was presented as if scientific research on human remains would come to an end (e.g. Walker, 2000). We now regularly return human remains to their communities of origin and the sky has not fallen in; science continues but in a more open and engaged way. Indeed, it is likely that when information discovered during research can be compared to willing participants from any community the benefit is likely to be greater.

When conducting research on human remains it is important to consider why the actual remains need to be used. Often remains are used as proxies for living communities but the matching of these groups is sometimes not as good as it could be. Remains are sometimes included because they are known about rather than because they are the best proxy available. Curators in museums have a responsibility to consider such issues before agreeing to access. Most museums, at least in European countries, ask for a project description and a justification for the remains which will be used in the study. This is essential and provides the ability to consider the ethics of the research proposed.

4.4   Ethical Models for Human Remains

It seems fairly clear that it would not be possible to use the same ethical model for all remains. We should look at how remains in museums can be cared for, displayed and research undertaken while still maintaining an ethical approach. One could have an overarching ethical statement and code of practice, as is seen currently in many museums and many professional organisations whose members study and care for human remains.

However, this can only be general guidelines. There are some excellent examples of these in the codes of the AAPA, BABAO, the British Ethnographic Society, American Academy for the Advancement of Science and many others. This does not, however, address the difficulties in working across the whole range of human remains and can still lead to disagreements with descendant communities. A more comprehensive and cooperative approach is required. This also needs to encompass the different world views on human remains which are discussed in Chapter 6. The view of some communities is that all remains from their region are ancestors, which makes achieving such an approach difficult. However, it should be possible to improve on the current position, and if the rules apply to all remains equally in a category then this might make it easier for them to be accepted – particularly if indigenous communities also have input in drawing them up. One forum for doing this is the World Archaeology Congress, which brings together experts researching human remains, as well as many other issues, and representatives of the indigenous communities from across the world. The opportunity to discuss and jointly propose motions to the congress has led to progress in this area. There are, however, few sets of rules laid down for what to consider when working with human remains in a more general and overarching way. One document that does address this is the United Kingdom's Department of Culture Media and Sport (DCMS) Guidance for Human Remains in Museums. In this a framework is set out which could be used as a model when considering how to approach these ethical problems. The Guidance document sets out the following and therefore gives a clear view on what should be considered.

1 Non-maleficence – doing no harm.
2 Respect for diversity of belief – including diverse religious, spiritual and cultural beliefs and attitudes to remains; tolerance.
3 Respect for the value of science – respect for the scientific value of human remains and for the benefits that scientific inquiry may produce for humanity.
4 Solidarity – furthering humanity through cooperation and consensus in relation to human remains.
5 Beneficence – doing good, providing benefits to individuals, communities or the public in general.

All the following models have these principles at their core. Two models are examined as these are the ones most usually considered when institutions put ethics at the centre of studying human remains.

Medical Model

Most medical models have at their heart the idea of consent (e.g. Human Tissue Act, 2004). This would make them easy to apply to the newly dead, and to the recently dead if close relatives can be identified, as it is then possible to ask permission to undertake research, display and to retain them in collections. However, descendants rapidly multiply and there would soon be such a large number that opinion would be as divided as in the general population.

It would be far more difficult to apply this model to the long dead or ancient dead as it would not be clear who should be consulted. The population of any region was much smaller in the past and so any individual from long ago is likely to have many thousands of descendants today. For example, someone alive in the Neolithic period in Britain about 5,000 years BP (Before Present) would probably be an ancestor of every person of European descent living today. This is about 450 million people, and obtaining any consensus for what to do would be impossible. However, getting an overview from the British population would be easier and attempts have been made for example by Historic England (2009).

The medical model also uses ethics committees to oversee whether or not the research should be allowed to take place. These committees scrutinise all the documents, including information to participants and consent forms. Such committees are routinely used not just in a medical setting but in universities when research will involve the participation of living people.

Ethics Committee

The role of an ethics committee is to scrutinise the research and see that it does not produce harm in those taking part. Such a panel could be used to look at the research to be undertaken on the recently dead and the long dead. The panels would most likely be either involved in the process undertaken as part of grant making or come from within the institution at which the research will be conducted. This would mean that in the case of museum collections the holding institution would undertake this ethical review. To do so fairly would mean canvassing any person who had a direct interest in the area, much the same as when consultations are held, and this would be particularly important for contentious remains such as those likely to be requested by home communities for return. This would allow input from descendant communities. In a country that has its own minority indigenous community then representatives of such communities should be members of the panel.

The NHM has set up both an ethics panel and a scientific panel for repatriation. This has worked well and provided a separate body to make the final recommendations to the Trustees (NHM, 2006). Something similar could be set up for very ancient remains to ensure that research is ethical and unlikely to be harmful to people living today. In many respects it is the harm to the living which can be the most difficult to deal with and is often forgotten when considering the ancient dead. For some cultures time and relationships are viewed differently to the standard Western model and these differing world views need to be considered (Jones & Harris, 1998).

4.5 Conclusions

There needs to be an understanding of what is meant by ethics and there must be more than just vague statements of intent. Ethical principles should be at the heart of any consideration of ethical standards. The principles set out in the DCMS guidance cover the main issues relating to human remains. These include doing no harm and respect for the beliefs of others including the value of science, working cooperatively and providing benefits for individuals, communities or the general public. If we work to such standards we will have provided an ethical basis for caring for human remains.

Questions

1 What do we mean by ethics?
   A Standards of right and wrong; what humans ought to do
   B Religious belief
   C How one feels about something
   D What is legal

2 Is ethics usually covered in courses and training?
   Yes
   No

3 What is today considered the most important point when dealing with human remains?

4 An action is ethical and moral if that action is part of an established trade or activity.
   True
   False

5 Are all human remains the same?
   Yes
   No

6 What are the four categories of human remains? Select all relevant.
   A The newly dead
   B The recently dead
   C The long dead
   D The ancient dead
   E All of the above

7 How does the age of the remains change public perception?

8 Working with remains is a right.
   True
   False

9 What should be considered when using remains in research? Select all that are relevant.
   A Proxy for living community
   B Have benefit or increase understanding
   C The easiest to gain access
   D Respect for the beliefs of others

10 What two models are most appropriate when considering inclusion of remains in research?

5   Good Practice in Curating Human Remains

In common with all museum and institution collections human remains need to be cared for using the most appropriate methods to ensure their safe storage, correct cataloguing and labelling, that appropriate access conditions are applied and that special consideration is given to the acquisition of new remains (Collections Trust, 2018). The worldwide standard for collections care is Spectrum, which is a set of standards dealing with all aspects of collections management. However, human remains are a special class of collection material (Roberts, 2013; Clegg & Long, 2015). As discussed in earlier chapters, human remains have a unique place in collections as they are the remains of people like ourselves who were once living and breathing. This gives human remains a distinction not found in other specimens. Human remains may also be governed by different rules depending on legislation that exists in a particular country. Much of the specifics of this legislation was discussed in Chapter 3. Here general best practice will be covered but any specific differences will be referred to as appropriate.

It is always best to have clear and concise policy and procedures in place for the care of human remains (Redfern & Bekvalac, 2013). This ensures that there is no ambiguity and that the policy and procedures are easy to comply with as everyone is certain what is meant. They should also as far as possible be applied to all classes of remains within the collection. There will be exceptions to this, for example, the Human Tissue Act (2004) in England requires that consent is obtained for the public display of remains from people who either donate their body for use after their death or who donate body parts during life. A good illustration of this is the case of tooth donation. At the Natural History Museum, London there is an ongoing project which collects the deciduous teeth from living children which have been shed as part of the normal maturation process. A consent form had to be developed to ensure that all options, including the possibility that the teeth might be displayed, were covered and consent for this was clear or that no consent for display was given. However, many of the teeth had been donated prior to the Human Tissue Act coming into force. All of the donation letters from earlier times were examined to ensure that if someone had placed restrictions on their donation that this was noted and could then be acted upon.

5.1 Policy and Procedures

It is essential that any institution holding human remains in its collection has a separate policy and procedures relating to all the eventualities that might occur when caring for, allowing access to or acquiring human remains (DCMS, 2004). The existence of such documents ensures that all staff are clear as to what is allowed and that those requesting access or wishing to deposit remains with the institution can understand the stages needed to allow such activities. This clarity prevents misunderstandings and potential problems, be they internal, external or reputational.

It is in general best to begin with a policy document. This should set out the broad principles under which you will work as a researcher and refer to any legislation as necessary. The policy should define what the institution classes as human remains, bearing in mind any legal constraints, give an overview of the make-up of the collection, including time periods covered, geographic regions, type of remains and the number of remains held. Each area of activity that might include human remains should be defined. These would normally include access to the collection; research that is permitted, including any destructive analysis; how remains are stored; how remains are documented; repatriation of remains; acquisition of remains; disposal other than through return to country of origin or direct descendants; filming and photography; and discussions with interested parties. It should also set out the roles, responsibilities and obligations of the museum staff involved in the care of the remains as well as a general outline of expectations from visitors. The policy document should outline the broad terms, with all the detail set out in the procedures document. The procedures document should cover in depth how each of the areas will be governed and what the actual steps are in undertaking any of the relevant actions.

Policy Document

All institutions need to have a human remains policy. In many cases this is required as part of government legislation or as part of the accreditation process museums undergo in various countries. The policy document sets out the overview of how the institution deals with human remains; this would also be true for many other types of policy. It may also make reference to more general policies such as documentation and destructive testing, as appropriate. Human remains need a separate policy because there are many different considerations unique to human remains which have to be discussed and dealt with.

Procedures Document

This is the how-to-do document, essentially a book of instructions, needed to ensure that there is consistency in the way each aspect relevant to the collection is dealt with and that the museum staff are clear on what they have to do and what needs to be considered before such matters as access are agreed.

Acquisitions

This section of the procedures document should explain the type of remains that will be considered for acquisition and the method to be used to ensure due diligence when any acquisition occurs. This section will be one that will most likely have different processes for different categories of remains as the sources and methods of acquisition may vary. It will set out the due diligence requirements to ensure that the acquisition of human remains is both legal and ethical. The level of documentation for this would be different for different categories of remains. If remains came from an archaeological dig then any permits/licences should accompany the donation; if from an existing collection then copies of the original donation letters should be available. If the remains are modern then any restrictions on, for example, public display should also accompany the donation. It should specify the types of remains that would be accepted. A museum could decide that it would not accept remains from an existing collection that might be subject to repatriation, for example. It might also set out the time periods or locations from which remains would be accepted. For example, the Museum of London primarily accepts human remains from the greater London area.

Access

This section should specify the types of access permitted. This would include research access – although this would also be expanded in the research permitted section – repatriation visits, visits by genetic descendants, public display and other public access to remains, including media usage. Each type of access should have its own process for gaining permission for the activity or visit. This should include usage by other departments in the museum, such as public engagement.

The process for each type of access should be set out, including who to approach, who makes the access decision, what information is required from the applicant – for example a request to view remains which are being claimed for repatriation might require either a letter from the First Nation Elders asking to arrange a viewing or this might come through the Embassy or High Commission of the home country – and the proposed date of the visit. Research access would normally require an outline of the proposed research, the experience of the researcher, why the remains requested are the most appropriate and the proposed dates of the visit. Having the date when the visit is planned is important as many museums have a very high number of requests for research access and so need to check that there will be space for the researcher at the proposed time. In repatriation cases the museum may stipulate that a particular number of staff is available and that they will have time to move the remains from storage to a suitable space to give privacy and dignity for the visit.

This section should also set out details of how remains are accessed during the visit. For research visits this should set out the number of individuals that can be taken from the store at a single time, whether more than one individual can be examined at the same time – not advisable unless all bones are clearly marked – and what to do if a problem occurs. It should also set out what each type of visitor can expect from the museum staff.

Types of Research Permitted

This section of the procedures document should set out the areas of research that are either permitted or for which the collection is most suitable. It should set out the conditions under which destructive analysis of all types can be considered. This might include the number of individuals that can be accessed for such research, the methods that can be used or not used and any special conditions that apply – for example, that photographs and perhaps casts must be made before any material is allowed to be extracted from the remains, or if available 3D scans of the remains. It might also set out the level of research that is permitted. For example, the NHM does not permit undergraduate-level research due to the high volume of requests from masters, PhD and postdoctoral researchers and the limited space available.

Storage of Remains

Most guidance on the care of human remains such as the DCMS Guidance (2004) gives very general advice on the storage of human remains. This usually involves suggesting that human remains are stored as single individuals as far as possible, that they are stored separately from other artefacts such as animal bones or mineralogy specimens and that they are stored in a way that is compatible with dignity and respect. This information should be included in the procedures document along with the type of storage materials to be used, the place of storage and the conditions under which the remains will be kept.

Documentation

All human remains should be fully documented to modern museum standards. This is of course an aspiration in many museums as collections will have been in the museum for varying lengths of time and in the past the level of documentation was almost at the whim of the curator since no agreed standards existed. At a minimum, the listing for the remains should give their geographic origin, the number and type of bones present, the donor and/or collector, the age and sex if available, whether the remains have been part of other institution collections and, for internal use, the location of the remains within the museum. The document should also state if a database is used and whether this is will be accessible to others through the internet. If the museum has the resources then a more complete set of data for each individual could be collected using methods outlined in Chapter 9.

Repatriation

This section should give the conditions under which a request for the return of remains would be considered. It should also make reference to any legislation and what this means for returning remains. Details of who to contact and the full process should be outlined, including how the authority of those making the claim is verified and, if the claim is being made through a third party, what information and authority will be accepted. The level of third-party involvement permitted would of course be up to the institution. Most institutions would rather work directly with the community but initially at least other organisations might be involved, or make the first approach. These could include the home government of the community making the claim or of an archaeological or other organisation such as a museum or institution mandated to assist with repatriation, as is the case in New Zealand. The method by which a decision is reached on whether or not to return should be outlined.

The methods used to provenance the remains claimed for return should be given and guidance as to the time scale. Information about the process after any decision to return is made should also be provided and the level of financial support the museum would offer. In most cases this is purely the work involved to ensure the provenance of the remains and the first part of the packing, even if community representatives actually pack themselves. If no further support is offered this should be stated in order to ensure there is no confusion, since repatriation is a very expensive business.

Any government legislation about repatriation or any guidance should be included. This is important if remains are from the home country.

Other Disposal

There will be times when remains have to be removed from collections for reasons other than repatriation. The conditions under which this would occur should be clearly set out. Many guidance documents such as that of the Department of Media Culture and Sport (DCMS, 2004) from the United Kingdom give examples of the type of conditions. This might include very badly damaged remains, transferring remains between institutions and unifying collections. If the remains are to be destroyed, as for example if massive damage occurred to them or they became contaminated, then the method of disposal should be given and how this decision would be reached.

Filming and Photography

Most guidance documents do not give any advice about filming and photography. It is usually best to have some information about the circumstances under which these activities could take place. This is important as there is an increasing desire by TV and film companies to use remains in documentaries and how the museum responds to media requests must be clear and unambiguous to ensure that only high-quality productions are given access.

Discussions

Discussions about human remains are usually in the context of repatriation claims and are part of the long negotiations that take place. However, many other people do on occasion want to discuss matters such as policy or research activities and it is wise to set out who to contact and the terms under which discussions can take place.

It also helpful to visitors if certain sections are set out separately as extracts which can be given to research visitors or claimants for the return of remains, for example, to help them understand what to expect from the museum and what the museum staff expect from them.

Day-to-Day Care

Human remains are rarely stored and then left and so the day-to-day care they receive is important. The training of human remains curators should cover the environmental conditions, the type of storage materials in use and the supervision of visitors.

Storage of Human Remains

In England and Wales the DCMS guidance document (2004) sets out the sort of standards expected for all aspects of the care of human remains. This is an excellent document which gives practical guidance to museum staff. However, what is best practice does change over time. This is particularly true when considering the type of storage material that might be used to protect human remains. Today there are many companies producing archival-quality boxes, tissue, card and bags in which remains can be stored. These range from custom-made boxes to basic boxes and bags (Figure 5.1). The storage within the boxes may also vary depending on the funds and the time available. A suggested minimum standard would be as follows based on University of Bradford guidance 2011:

1 All human remains should be stored in a separate space from other museum specimens. This can be as simple as separating out the human remains if the collection is small and ensuring that they are not interspersed with animal bones, for example. If money and space allow then provision of a separate bone store is ideal.

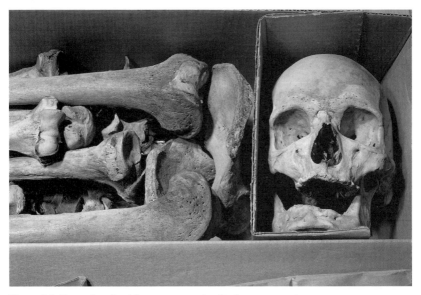

Figure 5.1 Example of good storage practice for human remains.
Credit: John B. Carnett/Bonnier Corporation/Contributor/Popular Science/Getty Images

2 All skeletal elements should if possible marked with a unique identifier, indicating the collection and skeleton number to which they belong; if not possible then all boxes and bags used for storage should be so marked.

3 Complete and partial skeletons to be bagged in re-sealable polythene bags according to anatomical region or skeletal element.

4 Where possible, each individual should be stored in an individual low-acid skeleton box. However, for very small or incomplete skeletons this may impractical. Where more than one individual is stored in a low-acid cardboard box, these should be separated from each other through the use of large re-sealable polythene bags or low-acid cardboard trays. In cases of very large or very fragile skeletons, individuals may be split between two boxes. In these cases, the boxes will be stored adjacent to each other in the store and will be labelled 1 of 2 and 2 of 2. Use skeleton boxes that have been designed to contain a large adult skeleton comfortably. Unusual pathological specimens may need to have special boxes to contain and support the human remains in such a way that large/fragile materials are not damaged.

5 Disarticulated or co-mingled remains cannot be stored as individuals. They should be stored in low-acid cardboard boxes according to site and context, where this is known.

6 Anatomical specimens, including those with pathological alterations, can be stored in cabinets or drawers to facilitate access for teaching; however these should be located in a secure room. The drawers should be lined with supporting foam and fragile specimens should be wrapped in acid-free tissue paper and placed in re-sealable polythene bags. Cabinets will be locked where practicable.

The use of such guidance will allow most institutions to comply with the local standards, which usually include separation of human remains from other specimens, separation of individuals and the treatment of remains with dignity and respect (e.g. DCMS, 2004).

Use of Human Remains in Public Display

When curators are asked to supply human remains for public display either as examples as part of a public lecture or in the temporary or permanent displays in the museum or other institution they should consider whether the use of the remains is essential to telling the story being presented. Human remains should only be used in such contexts if their use is integral to the display. They should never be used to shock, titillate or make a display 'sexy' or scary. Their role must be to educate and inform. There may be times when the use of casts is more appropriate; however, care is needed as sometimes the use of casts is very selective. For example, a US museum has a display of skulls illustrating human evolution and within this is a display showing the diversity within modern humans; real skulls have been used for all groups with the exception of Native Americans, which actually highlights the different treatment sometimes applied to remains from different communities. It would surely have been better to use casts for all groups if the use of real remains in one category would create problems.

Research Use of Remains

There should be a set of guidelines for all visitors as well as a copy of any policies that are relevant. This should be given to any research visitor at the outset of their visit. If the work space for visitors is away from that of the museum staff then a regular check should be made to ensure that the researcher is able to continue working and that they are complying with the museum's policies and procedures. If the curator is in a separate space then telephone extension numbers should be provided in case of difficulties. There should also be clear guidance on what to do if there is a problem. This can range from breakages to finding that the wrong remains are in a particular box.

If the visit is for the purpose of taking samples for destructive or transformative analysis, such as the removal of calculus, then it is preferable that the researcher is accompanied, at least at first, to ensure that they comply with the agreed methods and that there are no problems. It may be preferable for the curator to remove the relevant boxes of remains and place them in a separate space to ensure this. Although most researchers will happily comply with any restrictions placed on them there are sometimes cases where this has not been so and more remains than agreed are sampled or larger than agreed samples are taken.

Repatriation Visits

There are two types of repatriation visit. One is the visit during negotiations and the other is for the collection of remains. From a practical point of view these overlap to some extent. The following are suggested ways of dealing with repatriation visits.

1 If remains are to be shown to the Elders or Traditional Owners who are visiting then agreement in advance of the number of remains to be viewed is essential. This is particularly important when the museum holds a large number of remains, which can be time-consuming to remove from storage and overwhelming for the community representatives.

2 Any viewing should be in an area separate from the main storage zone and should give the Community Elders privacy to see the remains and talk to staff.

3 Viewing of the storage area can be agreed but should form part of a tour of the facility – more to see how remains are stored than to actually view them.

4 When the visit is for the physical return then a series of agreements need to be made in advance. These may be presented as a series of questions:

   4.1 Does the community want to hold a ceremony and if so how long will this take? What sort of ceremony will it be and what sort of space is required? This is important. If, for example, a smoking ceremony is being held then a space not fitted with sprinklers would be needed.

   4.2 Do the community wish to pack the remains for the journey themselves? Again it is important to know this in advance, particularly when large numbers of remains are being returned.

   4.3 Do the representatives want to be at the museum when the courier arrives and perhaps sign across the seals to satisfy themselves that no tampering occurs en route?

   4.4 Do they want press involvement and if so at what level? It could be a simple press release or it could be a press conference for local press, or if an important collection or event then national or international press.

   4.5 Do they want to film or photograph the process?

These are some of the things which need to be considered during any repatriation visit.

5.2   Other Issues

This chapter is an introduction to some of the issues that arise when curating human remains. Other issues are considered elsewhere in this book: for example, ethical and legal issues (Chapters 4 and 3, respectively). It is rarely the case that a museum or other institution is starting from scratch. However, as times and views change processes need to be updated in any institution. This is particularly important with human remains, which are such an emotive issue. One factor not discussed is the attitude of long-standing members of staff. These may be either other curators of human remains at the institution or researchers on the staff. They may also be colleagues in other areas or even the museum management. People do not always move seamlessly into new ways of thinking and working and often changes have to be approached in an inclusive manner rather than as a direct imposition. It is better to present changes in terms of legislative or changes in guidance and take other colleagues through step by step. This is a process similar to working with communities to ensure cooperation rather than conflict.

Questions

1 What is the worldwide standard for collections?
   A Spectrum
   B Human Tissue Act
   C NAGPRA
   D DCMS Guidance

2 Why do you need a separate policy and procedures for human remains?
   A So that museum staff are clear on what is allowed
   B It is the law that they exist
   C Management insists the museum has them
   D Part of museum bureaucracy

3 Which document is it best to start with?
   A Policy then procedures
   B Procedures then policy

    C Doesn't matter as long as they both exist

    D Not sure what these documents are

4 What should the policy document set out?

    A Broad principles under which the museum will work with human remains

    B Overview of collections

    C Outline of activities that might include human remains

    D Roles and responsibilities of staff

    E All of the above

5 Name the areas usually included in a procedures document.

6 Select the most appropriate methods for storing human remains.

    A Store as far as possible as separate individuals in low-acid boxes

    B Bag remains within box by anatomical region

    C Have a unique identifier for each individual

    D Co-mingled remains stored in low-acid box marked with site and context

    E Anatomical specimens stored in cabinets or drawers to allow access for teaching

    F store in separate lockable space

    G All of the above

7 Which reasons should never be the ones for including human remains in public display?

    A Shock the visitors

    B Make a talk 'sexy'

    C Be important in telling the story

    D To educate and inform

8 What questions should be asked of communities before a visit to view remains?

    A Do the community want to hold a ceremony?

    B Do the community want to pack the remains for repatriation themselves?

C Do the representatives want to be present when the remains are collected from the museum?

D Do they want press involvement?

E All of the above

9 If changes are needed to working practices how is it best to present them?

A As needed because of legislative or changes in guidance

B Imposed by management

C Because I say so

D Current practices are too old-fashioned

6 Other Belief Systems and the Care of Human Remains

When we discuss how to care for human remains there is general agreement that they should be treated with dignity and respect. However, although this implies a consensus, it is actually problematic as different cultures, religions and even subsets of these may have very different ideas as to what constitutes respectful treatment of the dead (Walker, 2000). In addition, practices within museums have changed over time so that what might have been deemed appropriate even twenty or thirty years ago would no longer be widely accepted (Ousely *et al.*, 2005). Even some indigenous communities have changed their attitudes to certain methods and techniques over this period and might now accept something once deemed unacceptable (Clegg & Long, 2015).

Furthermore, not all people within a culture or religious group might actively undertake all the practices but may see it as a good thing that these traditions are upheld (Pickering & Gordon, 2011). People often comment that they like to see a particular activity take place – for example, in the United Kingdom having a religious ceremony at a funeral, even though most people no longer attend church. This might seem to make it almost impossible to take account of other belief systems. However, there are methods by which an understanding can be reached. It is difficult for any institution that holds remains from many different regions of the world to fully appreciate the differences in belief systems and try to accommodate these within day-to-day working practice. Indeed most people would be unaware of traditional practices in other cultures except in the most general sense. Any conflict regarding how remains are treated usually surfaces during any negotiations surrounding repatriation or regarding the method of displaying remains in an exhibition. Having as the starting point that remains are always treated with dignity and respect, as would be the case for British human remains, helps to keep the focus on what we hold in common rather than the differences.

One of the main issues for indigenous communities when dealing with museums is the perception that remains from their community are treated differently to those of Europeans. There is often a perception that no research is carried out on European remains but only on indigenous remains. This belief does have foundation in fact: in the United States when remains were exhumed from burial sites, for example during development work, European remains were often reburied immediately while Native American remains were sent to a museum for study. Community representatives are often surprised when told that research is more often focused on other groups, particularly European and indeed British groups in British museums.

Another issue is that remains are often considered as being left on dusty shelves and not touched at all. Some human remains, particularly in smaller museums or institutions, may not be used for research but often this is because either the remains are not known to researchers or the institution has very limited resources to allow access. Furthermore, in most museums the idea that the remains would be stored on dusty shelves is not true. The majority of curators or, in larger institutions, conservation units would be horrified at the idea of remains not being stored correctly (see Chapter 5 for a fuller discussion of this issue). Most institutions actively conserve the remains in their collections and strive to achieve the best possible standards of care. The description of remains on dusty shelves is generally one fostered by the media when they want to convey something spooky or scary about human remains or to suggest that the programme researchers have discovered something unknown to the museum staff. It is usually the first thing that is raised in an interview by the press and always has to be explained. A version of this view can even be seen in the Working Group on Human Remains set up in 2001 to look at how human remains, particularly from former colonies, were stored (Palmer, 2003). The problems with this view and why the working group held it are discussed in Chapter 8.

During 2011 the NHM hosted two Australians on visiting fellowships under a knowledge exchange programme. One was from the Australian Aboriginal community and the other a Torres Strait Islander. They worked alongside museum staff and were trained in many of the more straightforward curatorial tasks. In turn they taught the museum staff about Australian Aboriginal and Torres Strait belief systems and the Aboriginal world view of the dead. They took part in normal museum activities in the same way as museum staff. During their visit the NHM was running a project to re-box part of the collection comprising Romano-British remains dating to the Iron Age. The fellowship holders kept a record book of their work to facilitate writing their final reports. One of them wrote that she was boxing non-indigenous remains, which would have been true had she been in Australia. I asked her to think about where the remains were from and where they were stored. It suddenly dawned on her that these too were indigenous remains and that indigenous simply meant the original inhabitants of a location, despite definitions of indigenous as the dispossessed being widely accepted in many publications (e.g. Stanley, 2007). It was a revelation for both fellowship holders and changed their perspective on human remains.

The issue of storage is also one which visits to these areas by indigenous community representatives can help to resolve. Tours of the storage area

Figure 6.1 The author and fellowship holders at the NHM. © The Trustees of the Natural History Museum London

and the working spaces are usually enough to show them that the remains are not abandoned and forgotten. Show-and-tell sessions with the remains also provide information which illustrates the research that has been undertaken and the knowledge and skill of the collection management staff. These times also allow the community to see that their ancestors have contributed to scientific knowledge, including answering questions which have a relevance today. Many communities then realise that the museum staff do treat the remains with dignity and respect and that although it is perhaps not exactly as they would wish, the remains are not treated differently to those from the country in which the museum belongs.

6.1   Who Decides on How Remains Are Stored and Treated?

To some extent it has to be the holding institution that decides on how remains are stored and treated since often they are constrained by legislation, government guidance and local custom (see Chapters 3, 5 and 8). In many respects following best practice is a good way of also answering the concerns of indigenous communities. In the Department of Culture, Media and Sport's Guidance (2004) and in the Standards for Human Remains (Buikstra & Ubelaker, 1994) emphasis is placed on storing remains as individuals as far as possible. The use of remains for research also addresses another issue often raised by indigenous communities, who are often convinced that the remains are articulated skeletons left hanging in cupboards. Although many museums and universities have some articulated skeletons, often for comparative purposes, such remains are less useful for research. Showing people the storage facilities often helps dispel this idea. It is also important that when remains are used in public events, community representatives as well as the general public see the curator, scientist or other staff member handling the remains with respect. Again this means following best practice, such as wearing gloves when handling the remains, being calm and sensitive when talking about remains and not displaying remains in any way which could give rise to ridicule.

It is possible to accommodate some aspects of beliefs within the standards of care usually accepted in Western museums. Often small changes in storage or boxing can be used. It might be as simple as changing the orientation of the skull within the storage box. This may necessitate a

new support being put in the box but can change how the community feel
about the methods used. It might be by segregating male and female
remains, although it is necessary to remind the representatives of the
indigenous groups or nations that often the actual sex of the remains is
unknown, the listed sex being the best estimate using standard techniques.
It might also be the position within the storage area that needs attention.
Some First Nation groups find particular locations more or less acceptable.
For example, some islands within the Torres Strait consider a high location
more acceptable because ancestral skulls would historically have been
placed high in trees or caves. Other groups prefer lower levels so that
remains are closer to the earth. Some communities might traditionally
mark the remains with red ochre. At the NHM boxes from one such
community were marked with red ochre and small pieces were placed in
wrapping within the boxes at the request of community members. It is
therefore important to talk and listen to representatives of any community
you are working with so that if possible within other constraints it is
possible to accommodate at least some of their wishes in respect of storage.
It is also essential to ensure that best practice is used when storing and
using remains. Good storage does not necessarily equate to spending large
sums of money (see Chapter 5 for details).

One issue that is important here is the need to hold discussions with the
representatives of the communities. There needs to be a flow of information between the museums and the communities involved. This applies
not only to repatriation but to wider perceptions within even the home
country of the museum. Hosting seminars or attending those held by other
institutions and organisations, as well as finding ways of discussing issues
in an informal setting, are important. A seminar held by the Australian
High Commission in 2007 during which Bin-Sallik spoke about the world
view of Australian Aboriginal people was seminal in beginning the NHM's
understanding of the perspective of both Aboriginal and Torres Strait
Island peoples. Although beliefs in Australia are diverse, being shaped by
the exact environment the clan lives in, she outlined the three commonal-
ities in the belief systems of all Australian clans: dreaming, land and
kinship. These three provide the laws, customs, social cohesion and identity for the clans. Her talk highlighted several issues which shed light on
concerns from indigenous communities that the museum staff had found
hard to understand. The first was the Australian First Nation view that

time was cyclical. This gives a more direct connection with ancestors, who in essence are waiting to be reborn, than the Western idea of linear time. Another issue that had not been clear was the importance of kinship and how kinship extended through generations, conferring rights, responsibilities and obligations from each generation to the others. These views are similar to those held by other communities. For example, the idea of kinship as described above is essentially the same as the view of the Maoris in New Zealand. This highlighted the importance of repatriation to Australian and other communities in that they were fulfilling their obligations to ancestors who would be reborn. The importance of mortuary rituals was also emphasised by an extended period of mourning. It is essential that the rituals are followed in order to ensure that the ancestor passes to the spirit world and does not linger in the physical world, where they might be prevented from completing their journey. For remains held in museums, the living members of a clan have no way of knowing how much of the rituals, if any, have taken place; the ancestor may be trapped between worlds. In effect they are merely asking for the dignity owed to all those who have lost loved ones: to be able to bury their dead. Other talks such as those held by the World Archaeology Congress give much information about the world view of the diverse communities of indigenous peoples around the world. The opportunity that such conferences and seminars give to begin to understand others' world views is invaluable. They also offer the chance to speak to members of different groups and begin to build understanding.

Having indigenous people resident at an institution for an extended period can also help to break down barriers. For the NHM the fellowships the museum hosted in 2011 were also significant in this context. Usually meetings between museum staff and indigenous peoples are necessarily relatively brief, because of the distances involved and costs inherent in travel. The fellowships allowed them to work together and interact on a more mundane level than is usually possible. This meant that normal working relationships were established and friendships formed, leading to more and deeper discussions about human remains and other aspects of life than would normally occur. One relevant factor was that both fellows were female, as was the majority of the NHM human remains unit. This meant the 'women's business' was easier to discuss than in mixed company and built greater trust. It was also surprising how similar female views were cross-culturally. Having listened to Bin-Sallik's talk, there was a framework of understanding on the NHM staff side which could be built on during discussions with the fellowship holders. All of the above are my interpretations and understandings of Aboriginal belief and culture. It may not be wholly correct but gives a flavour of their beliefs and, more importantly, how a European might understand them.

6.2   Public Display of Human Remains

In general human remains should only be displayed if their presence is an integral part of the story being told. Human remains should never be used to shock, titillate or purely to generate interest. Within many Western societies there is in fact an expectation that human remains will be displayed in museums. Surveys such as Historic England (2009) and Cambridge County Council (2009) have shown that this is seen as acceptable in the United Kingdom even among those who like to see remains ultimately reburied. This stance has been clear in other countries, including the United States and Canada, despite large indigenous communities in both countries. In New Zealand, where there is reluctance to display Maori and Moriori remains, an exhibition on ancient Egypt sparked widespread debate as to whether displaying other people's ancestors was hypocritical or if this was acceptable where they were from vanished civilisations (New Zealand Herald, 2006). Even though the present-day Egyptian population had no objection to such exhibitions, there was debate as to whether it was defensible. It presented an interesting insight into how the ancient dead from lost cultures are viewed even by those who wish the return of ancestral remains.

When human remains are to be displayed it is crucial that any sensitivities are addressed. In some cultures it is not acceptable to see the dead. For example, both Inuit and Australian Aboriginal people do not refer to the dead for long after the event and have traditionally shunned the burial site (Meehan, 1971), and even in modern Western societies some people are squeamish about seeing remains unexpectedly (DCMS, 2004). It is therefore important that notices are erected to inform visitors that they may see the remains of long-dead people. This is now done almost automatically in museums in places such as Australia but is less common

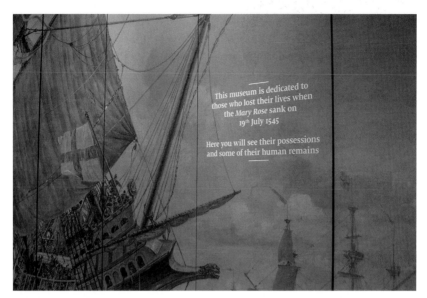

Figure 6.2 Mary Rose entrance display showing warning that human remains on display.
© The Mary Rose Trust

in European museums. It should become part of planning for an exhibition, since today museums are rarely only catering for the people who live
nearby. Many museums, especially those in large cities, have visitors from
all around the world. It is essential to be sensitive to the feelings and beliefs
of others by giving warning that human remains are present. This allows
the visitor to be in control of what they see and not to be presented
unexpectedly with something they might find shocking. This does not
mean that the warnings need to elicit fear. Among the many treasures
brought up from the *Mary Rose*'s resting place on the sea bed off the local
coast, the Mary Rose Museum in Portsmouth, United Kingdom, has
displayed the remains of some of the crew. At the entrance there is a sign
which dedicates the museum to the crew who died on the day the ship
sank and also lists the number of dead and states that some of their
remains are on display (Figure 6.2). The remains themselves are exhibited
in a separate area which does not have to be entered as part of the tour.
The remains of seven people are displayed alongside the reconstruction of
what they would have looked like in life. It makes the whole exhibition
poignant and somehow personal.

Another exemplary exhibition was the London Bodies displayed in the gallery at the Wellcome Trust (2018). This exhibition brought dignity to the remains as well as telling the story of the people buried in London over the centuries. The skeletons were laid out on special tables which supported the bones without being intrusive, and the lighting was deliberately kept low. Visitors tended to talk in hushed tones and there was nothing to detract from the skeletons of these long-dead Londoners (Bekvalac, pers. comm.). The publicity made it very clear that skeletons were on display and it was unlikely that anyone would have visited unwittingly.

Both of the exhibitions cited above are of people from the country in which the exhibition took place. If one wanted to use human remains from any other place then consultation with families or the relevant community would be essential to ensure that those with ancestors in the exhibition did not feel that they were not being considered and that consent was not sought. It is important within the context of exhibitions to treat all human remains in the same way. At the Smithsonian there is an exhibit on human evolution and the response of modern humans to the environment in which they live. All the major regions of the world are represented by a human skull, except for the skull of a Native American, which is a cast. It is very obviously a cast. If it was deemed unacceptable to display a Native American then for consistency all the skulls should have been casts so as not to draw attention to the discrepancy. In some respects this has reinforced the idea that some remains are treated differently.

6.3   Use of Remains in the Media

Human remains are often used in both press and television to explain research, report on finds, advertise or review exhibitions and inform the public on other aspects of human remains such as repatriation. Many cultures have prohibitions on showing even photographs of people who are dead (AIJA, 2013). Similar precautions to those for public display should be taken, even though in most countries there is little or no legislation on the use of remains in photography.

The most important concern again is to talk to the people involved. This prevents anything being a shock. It is usually in the context of repatriation that the publishing of photographs is problematic. Many communities would rather that no photographs of the remains themselves were used. Institutions are generally willing to not use photographs of the remains and may instead use stock footage of non-contentious remains, for example to illustrate a technique that was important in defining the identity of any individual within the ancestral group.

In other circumstances the programme should flag that it is about human remains and the institution should ensure that its policy regarding handling, display and suchlike is followed.

In a repatriation context it is better to show the packed shipping cases rather than the remains. In one repatriation at the NHM the news programme wanted to show some of the techniques we used. Human remains were used as illustration but they were British remains and a caption on the screen made this clear.

6.4   Conclusions

It is difficult to accommodate different belief systems if museum staff do not know what these involve. A dialogue with any community, including the various members of one's own country, is essential if ill-will and hurt feelings are to be avoided. Simple changes in location or position can ease matters, as can signage in exhibitions and events. This may seem as if other voices are interfering but the bad publicity and reputational damage that unwittingly causing offence can generate cannot be over-stated.

Questions

1 Why is it important to have a single standard for treating remains in a collection?

   A Easier to remember

   B Shows that all remains are treated with the same dignity and respect

   C Legal requirement

   D It's in the procedures document, not my job to decide

2 Why is allowing tours by indigenous groups to storage areas important?

 A Allows groups to see how remains are stored

 B Stops worries about remains as articulated skeletons

 C Part of museum policy

 D The home government asked for this

3 What constraints exist that might prevent fully following other belief systems?

 A Legal requirements

 B Safe storage of remains

 C Health and safety

 D Requirements too difficult

4 List examples of small changes that can be made in storing human remains to take account of other beliefs.

5 What factor is important to both Australian Aboriginal peoples and Maoris?

 A Kinship

 B Geographic location

 C Responsibility to ancestors

 D Land rights

6 Why is it important to signpost the presence of human remains in an exhibition?

 A Political correctness

 B Sensitivity to beliefs and feelings of others

 C Allows people to know what is in the exhibition

 D Stops people being shocked

7 In repatriation situations which of the following should be allowed in media coverage?

 A The actual remains being returned

 B Examples of non-contentious remains to illustrate techniques

 C No pictures at all

 D What the community is comfortable with

8 Why is dialogue with communities so important?

7 A History of Repatriation

Requests for the return of human remains from museums and other institutions are often considered a relatively new phenomenon. In the context of asking for all remains affiliated to a particular community it probably dates back to the 1970s (Fforde & Hubert, 2006). However, the call for remains of known individuals to be returned to families and their home community is not (Walker, 2000; Fforde & Hubert, 2006). Many indigenous people expressed a wish that their bones should not be placed in a museum during the period when remains were being collected in the nineteenth and early twentieth centuries. In many cases these wishes were ignored by the colonial settlers in their scramble to take custody of the remains, often to send them to the United Kingdom or other colonial powers to enhance their standing and prestige as being the person or people responsible for sending them 'home'. Several specific cases are detailed below as examples of this. Famous people or those with special interest were also taken and displayed, often against their own or their family's wishes. There are many examples of this and a selection is discussed below. This was not only the case for remains from indigenous communities; people from the home country were also collected in a similar fashion, generally without consent from either them or their families.

Many famous individuals or those from allegedly near-extinct communities were sent to museums to form part of their collections. The reasons for this were varied, but one common issue is that being displayed in a museum would not have been agreed by either the persons themselves or their families. The remains were often stolen from their graves after burial or even openly taken despite the objections of family (e.g. individuals such as Truginini). There was an implicit acknowledgement of this by the collectors who spoke of having to collect at night or in the face of local protest (Walker, 2000). This was not only an issue for indigenous remains; many other individuals were kept in museums, from other parts of the world but also from the home country. This was especially true for exceptional cases and two are discussed here: Charles Bryne (the Irish Giant) and Joseph Merrick (the Elephant Man).

7.1   Famous and Contentious Human Remains in Museums

Truginini

Truginini was regarded as the last Tasmanian Aboriginal. This is of course untrue but was widely accepted at the time and into more recent times. She was part of a small group of Aboriginal people who had been with George Augustus Robinson at Oyster Bay and later Flinders Island (Plomley, 1987). They had accompanied him when he returned to mainland Australia, but later returned to Tasmania. As each of the group died there was an unseemly rush to take possession of that person's body and remove organs and other body parts in the name of 'scientific research', as had happened to Willian Laney, another member of the group (Fforde & Hubert, 2006). Truginini had seen this and did not want it to happen to her. Despite her well-known objection to being put in a museum, on her death the surgeons clamoured to have access to her body and it was eventually placed in Hobart Museum, where it was displayed until 1947 (Fforde & Hubert, 2006), when it was removed to storage after public protests, especially from Tasmanian Aboriginal people. Only in 1976 was her body given back by the museum. Her remains were cremated and her ashes scattered in the D'Entrecasteaux Channel, near her birthplace, almost 100 years after her death (Morris, 2017).

Ishi

Ishi was probably the last of his tribe, the Yahi, when he was found in California. He was taken to the Natural History Museum in San Francisco and was both an exhibit and a research assistant. The anthropologist he worked with knew that asking a name in Yahi society was impolite and Ishi himself said he had no name as there was no one to say it. Ishi means man in the Yahi language. He lived at the museum for five years (Kroeber,

2002). After his death his friends and colleagues at the museum tried to prevent his body from being autopsied because in Ishi's culture the body should remain whole. However the medics insisted, and not only conducted an autopsy but removed his brain and sent it to the Smithsonian. Ishi was cremated along with his favourite and most important possessions. His brain and ashes were returned in 2000 to descendants of the Redding Rancheria and Pit River tribes, part of the Yani tribes – the closest survivors of Ishi's tribe (Kroeber, 2002).

Yagan

Yagan lived in the area of Perth and when Europeans first arrived he was friendly with them and was a well-known local figure (Hasluck, 1967). However, encounters with the settlers became difficult, with disputes over food and other resources, and there were many clashes. Yagan was outlawed and eventually killed by a former friend, probably for the £30 reward, worth about £3,000 today (Hasluck, 1967). His head was cut off after death and sent to England. During the 1950s Yagan's tribe, the Noongar, began a search for his remains (Mcglade, 1998). They were eventually located in an unmarked grave in Liverpool. All graves in Victorian and municipal cemeteries in the United Kingdom have a grave plan so it is possible to locate a grave even when it isn't marked on the ground (Rutherford, 2008). The remains were returned to Australia in 1997, 160 years after his death (Stumpe, 2005).

King Badu Bonsu II

King Badu Bonsu II, the ruler of the Ahanta tribe in present-day Ghana, decapitated two Dutch emissaries and decorated his throne with their heads. In 1898, in retaliation for this, he was beheaded by Dutch soldiers and his head sent to Holland. Ghana had always wanted the King's head returned but it could not be located. King Bonsu's head was found stored in a jar of formaldehyde in a Dutch museum. Ghana immediately asked for the return of the King's severed head and, in July 2009, members of the Ahanta flew to The Hague and, after more than 150 years, took the head back to Ghana (BBC, 2009).

The Hottentot Venus

Sarah 'Saartjie' Baartman was brought to Europe from South Africa, initially to Britain and later in France, and was exhibited in shows under the title of the Hottentot Venus. She died in 1815 and her body was dissected and then displayed at the Musee de l'homme in Paris (Qureshi, 2004). Calls for her return began in the 1940s, and interestingly the tone of the museum is familiar to all those who have worked in repatriation: the curator at the Musee de l'homme stated 'we never know what science will be able to tell us in the future. If she is buried, this chance will be lost . . . for us she remains a very important treasure' (Qureshi, 2004, p. 246). This was a frequent refrain in the past and continues to be so even today. Her remains were exhibited in the Musee de l'homme until 1974 when public pressure forced her removal from display. There was a long and difficult negotiation for her return after apartheid ended and her body was eventually returned to South Africa in 2002 (The Guardian, 2002). She was buried near her birthplace almost 200 years after her birth (Qureshi, 2004).

Pemulwuy

The head of Pemulwuy is probably one of the earliest remains recorded as being sent from Australia to Britain. Pemulwuy and his tribe give lie to the idea that there was little resistance to the arrival of Europeans and he was regarded by the Governor as a pest. He was outlawed and had a price on his head. He was killed and his head cut off to prove he was dead. Philip King, the Governor of New South Wales, sent the head to Joseph Banks. It was supposedly given to Mr Hunter's Museum – at least that is what Banks told Governor King (Chambers, 2007). However, the original entry was for two heads, listed as coming from Tahiti. They were not donated by Banks but by a colleague and relative of his. Several years later this entry was changed to show that the heads were from Australia.

The donor, Everard Home, was a member of staff at the museum. At the time of donation the museum had just been purchased by the Royal College of Surgeons (RCS) in London and forms the nucleus of its current museum. The last reference to the heads in the college's documents is in 1818. There is no record of what happened to the remains and no means of identifying the head, which may have been skeletonised. During World

War II the college was heavily bombed and a large number of museum specimens were destroyed. It is not clear from the college records how many items were lost. After the war, and in view of the problems caused by the bomb damage, a large number of remains were offered to the Natural History Museum. The head is not listed in this transfer and no documentation exists for it at the NHM. There have been many attempts to have Pemulwuy's head returned to Australia. However, as no documentary evidence exists and no remains are catalogued under this name it is impossible to identify any potential candidates as Pemulwuy. The Natural History Museum has agreed that when the provenance of the human remains affiliated to New South Wales is undertaken then a full provenance exercise will be undertaken. Despite this, repeated pressure is applied. There is a misunderstanding within Australia, where it is believed that there are remains which could potentially be Pemulwuy. No possible remains have ever been identified by any of the institutions involved, however, despite frequent searches of their records.

Geronimo

In common with many Apaches, Geronimo had a long history of resisting both European and Mexican settlers. He continued this even after other leaders such as Cochise had made peace. From 1881 he waged what is considered to be the last of the Indian wars. For over five years he raided and fought. He finally surrendered in 1886 and was held prisoner with the rest of his group for twenty-seven years (Barrett, 1906). He died in 1909 from complications of pneumonia brought on by hypothermia after falling from his horse and spending the night out in the cold in winter (New York Times, 1909). Just before he died he told his nephew that he should have fought to the last man and never surrendered (Barrett, 1906). He was buried in the Apache Indian Prisoner of War Cemetery at Fort Sill Oklahoma. It has been suggested that his skull and some other bones and some of the grave goods were removed by members of a Yale Secret Society, Skull and Bones, that served at Fort Sill in World War I. In 1986 a letter with a copy of a 1918 register for the society showing his skull as an entry was sent to the San Carlos Apache Chairman (Leach & Levy, 2014). The Chairman had a meeting with society officials, who denied that the skull was in their collection and claimed that it was a hoax.

The story keeps resurfacing when the 1986 letter and its copy of the register entry are seen by a new generation. In 2009 a lawsuit was filed on behalf of Geronimo's descendants, but as there is no hard evidence it was unsuccessful. The chair of the Apache tribe now regards the letter as a hoax (New York Times, 2009).

Pocahontas

During Anglo-Indian hostilities in 1613 Pocahontas was captured by the British and held for ransom. During her captivity she converted to Christianity and when ransomed refused to leave the British settlement. She married John Rolfe in 1614 and in 1616 the Rolfes, with their young son, travelled to England in the hope of gaining further investment in Jamestown. She was presented as a civilised 'savage' and became something of a celebrity, even attending the Royal Court at Whitehall (Mossier, 1996). The Rolfes began their journey home to America in 1617 but Pocahontas died of unknown causes at Gravesend at the beginning of the voyage. She was buried in St George's Church Gravesend. The exact location of her grave is unknown as the church was destroyed in a fire in 1727 but it was thought to be in the chancel. There have been many attempts to find her grave and the United States Congress even passed a resolution asking for her return for the American Bicentenary. Although her grave has not been located, there is some evidence that after the fire all the bones found were buried in a single grave as it was impossible to identify them individually at the time.

Yemmerrawanne

In 1792 Governor Philips returned to London bringing with him two Aboriginal men he had captured with the intention that they tell him about Aboriginal life, culture and kinship. His intention in bringing them to England was to show that it was possible to 'civilise' the Australians and in doing so live peacefully with them. Bennelong probably accompanied him partly through coercion and partly through kinship bonds that may have been formed as a survival mechanism by the captured Aboriginal people (Fullagar, 2009). Yemmerrawanne was only about sixteen when captured. During his stay in London he died, probably from a lung infection such as pneumonia, and was buried at Eltham in Kent (Fullagar,

2009). His grave is still in the churchyard there. Although there have been attempts to exhume and repatriate his body they have not been successful. The most prominent attempt was as part of a project conceived by the Australian-born UK barrister Geoffrey Robinson. This project was to re-inter Governor Arthur Philip in Sydney. Yemmerrawanne's remains would also have been returned and reburied in a large monument in an act of reconciliation (Robertson, 2007). The plan was unsuccessful partly because Aboriginal people were not happy with it, but mostly because of the inability to find Philip's remains in his burial place. There have been other efforts and it is surprising that none have been successful. Only permission from the church authorities and import permission from the Australian quarantine authority would be needed.

Charles Byrne

He is better known as the Irish Giant. Between 1781 and 1782 he was part of Cox's museum which exhibited strange and wonderful things. He was exhibited as being over 8ft tall but his skeleton suggests he was about 7ft 7ins in height. He became very famous but died from the effects of excessive alcohol consumption aged twenty-two in 1782. He did not want his body to be dissected or exhibited in a museum, and he arranged to be buried at sea (Royal College of Surgeons, 1831). However, John Hunter was keen to acquire him for his museum and bribed the sailors to give him his body, which is still exhibited in the Hunterian Museum at the Royal College of Surgeons, London. In 1909, examination showed he had a pituitary tumour which was thought to have given him his great height. He came from a normal-sized family.

There have been calls for his reburial (see Muinzer, 2013), but in 2011 British and German researchers determined the cause of Byrne's giganticism. They extracted DNA from Byrne's teeth and found that he had a rare mutation that is involved in pituitary tumours. The researchers also found that four contemporary families living in Northern Ireland which have a history of related pituitary disorders also carried this muta-tion (Muinzer, 2013). These are probably Byrne's closest living relatives, and they decided that his remains should stay in the museum for further study. However, in 2018 the RCS agreed to look again at burying his remains (The Guardian, 2018).

Joseph Merrick

Joseph Merrick is better known as the Elephant Man. Abandoned when his father remarried after his mother's death, he contacted a showman famous at the time as a way out of the terrible situation in a Victorian workhouse. He was robbed by the showman and left alone in Belgium during a continental tour. When Merrick returned to London alone and with no money he was arrested as a vagrant (Quigley, 2001). He had been in communication with and been examined by Dr Treves at the Whitechapel hospital. The police found Treves's card in Merrick's pocket and contacted him. Treves took him to hospital and nursed him back to health. He lived in safety at the hospital for several years. He died in 1890 aged twenty-seven. Merrick's body was retained under the Anatomy Act and was not claimed by his family. Treves dissected Merrick's body and took plaster casts of his head and limbs. He took skin samples – which were later lost during World War II – and mounted his skeleton, which remains in the pathology collection at the Royal London Hospital (Quigley, 2001). Although the skeleton has never been on public display, there is a small museum dedicated to his life, housing some of his personal effects.

The exact cause of Merrick's deformities is unclear. The dominant theory throughout much of the twentieth century was that Merrick suffered from neurofibromatosis type I. In 1986, a new theory emerged that he had Proteus syndrome. In 2001 it was proposed that Merrick had suffered from a combination of neurofibromatosis type I and Proteus syndrome. DNA tests conducted on his hair and bones have proven inconclusive.

There have been some attempts by various groups, including disability rights and the City of Leicester, for his burial but the museum maintains that it is in contact with his nearest descendants and has their permission for retention.

7.2   A More Recent History of Repatriation

The United States

In the United States the repatriation movement started as a civil rights (later human rights) issue (Ousely *et al.*, 2005). During rescue archaeological excavations it was widely thought that when Native

American remains were discovered they were taken to a museum for study, while European remains were quickly reburied (Walker, 2000). This may or may not have been true, but the perception was the important issue and all the arguments from the time do nothing to allay these fears by either denying it or by saying, as was probably the case, that both sets of remains were treated the same, with both going for further study (Walker, 2000). The long history of poor treatment and broken promises had led to a situation where only the worst possible outcome could be believed (Bieder, 2000).

In the United States concerned academics also had a part to play in increasing interest in the repatriation of remains from museums (Lovell, 2007) Native American Nations were encouraged to see the remains in museums in the same light as those recently excavated, often not telling them that collections also contain large numbers of European remains and thus encouraging the view that this was a discriminatory practice rather than the fate of most excavated remains (Ferguson *et al.*, 1996).

In 1989 the National Museum of the American Indian Act (NMAIA) was passed by Congress, this established the Museum of the American Indian and also required that the Smithsonian Institute inventory its Native American human remains as well as artefacts and consider repatriation to federally recognised Indian tribes and Hawaiian organisations. In 1990 a further law, the Native American Graves Protection and Repatriation Act (NAGPRA), was passed. This required federal agencies and institutions receiving federal funding to return cultural items to lineal descendants and affiliated tribes and Hawaiian organisations. Cultural items include human remains, funerary objects, sacred objects and objects of cultural patrimony. A programme of federal grants assists in the repatriation process and the Secretary of the Interior has the power to impose civil penalties on museums that fail to comply (NAGPRA, 1990). NAGPRA also set up procedures to deal with the inadvertent discovery or planned excavation of Native American cultural items on federal or tribal lands. While these provisions do not apply to discoveries or excavations on private or state lands, the collection provisions of the Act may apply to Native American cultural items if they come under the control of an institution that receives federal funding.

Lastly, NAGPRA makes it a criminal offence to traffic in Native American human remains without right of possession or in Native American cultural items obtained in violation of the Act. Penalties for a first offence may be up to twelve months' imprisonment and a $100,000 fine. For the first time Native Americans had the legal right to have ancestral remains returned to them and protection for newly discovered and disturbed remains. Interestingly, it is not an offence to buy and sell other human remains within the United States.

Australia

The repatriation movement in Australia grew from two areas: the need for political and legal rights for the original inhabitants of Australia. This again was a civil rights issue, and concerned the few high-profile individuals whose remains had been placed in museums against their express wishes (Pickering & Gordon, 2011). The legal status of the Aboriginal population of Australia was until fairly recently on a par with the native flora and fauna. Indeed, Aboriginal affairs in many states were dealt with by the Department of Agriculture or the National Parks Service (Fforde, 2004). Until 1967 they were not counted as part of the Australian population, for example during census taking. It was only in 1962 that they received the right to vote in federal elections. They had theoretically at least had the right to vote in state and local elections since the Australian citizenship act of 1949, although in practice in some states it was as late as 1962 before this was properly provided for (Galligan & Roberts, 2004).

Federal legislation has since been enacted covering land rights, discriminatory practices, financial assistance and preservation of cultural heritage. The other aspect of the constitutional change, enabling Aboriginal people to be counted in population statistics, has led to clearer evaluations of the desperate state of Aboriginal health. In Australia there are no federal laws that require the repatriation of Aboriginal and Torres Strait Islander remains and artefacts to culturally affiliated communities. However, each state or territory in the Australian Commonwealth has its own laws regulating this (Australian Federal Government, 2006).

These changes, and the fight for them, encouraged a growing confidence in the Aboriginal community and activists began to ask for the return of human remains from museums both at home and overseas, particularly in the United Kingdom.

Museums and universities in Australia were at first resistant but as laws were enacted in different states the return of both human remains and artefacts began to occur. Today the majority of aboriginal remains in Australian institutions are those for which provenance is poor.

New Zealand

The position in New Zealand is somewhat different to that in the United States and Australia. In New Zealand there is a more collaborative attitude built on long-standing treaties and mutual respect. The return of remains from New Zealand institutions is based on the Treaty of Waitanga, which is the governing concept behind the Constitution of New Zealand and government relationships with the Maori people (New Zealand Government, 1840). There are also a number of Acts of Parliament in New Zealand that give a legal framework for the treatment of archaeological sites, including any human remains (Buckley & Petchey, 2018) Before 1993 Maori were consulted as appropriate before any excavations took place; however after this time the 1993 Heritage Act made it a duty recognise Maori interests and in effect gave the Maori Heritage Council the right to decide what happens (Ruckstahl et al., 2016).

Interest in New Zealand remains from overseas was sparked by the sale of a Toi Makai (a tattooed head) in 1988 by the auction house Bonhams (Stumpe, 2005) and by the exhibition on Maori culture at the Te Papa Museum in the 1980s (http://collections.tepapa.govt.nz/object/31). Both these events brought into focus that human remains and Maori artefacts were held in museums both in New Zealand and overseas. The New Zealand Government mandated the Te Papa Museum to act on its behalf and inventory New Zealand human remains and artefacts held at home and overseas (http://collections.tepapa.govt.nz/about/repatriation).

The United Kingdom

As with the United States and Australia there was initially massive resistance to the idea of repatriation by the UK scientific academic community who worked with human remains and associated artefacts. There was a similar response from those in the humanities as in other countries (e.g. Foley, 2003; Lahr, 2003; Stringer, 2003; The Times, 2006; Jenkins, 2008).

During the 1990s there were many representations from indigenous communities but these were often from activist groups or a very small number of communities. Although the Natural History Museum, for example, received over thirty enquiries these were from fewer than six communities. Many enquiries were either from organisations such as Foundation for Aboriginal and Islander Research Action (FAIRA) or from individuals claiming to represent all the indigenous populations. There were returns during this period but these tended to be from smaller local or private museums. They included the Royal College of Surgeons Museum in London, and Manchester University Museum (The Independent, 2003), the Wellcome Trust (2018) and several local authority museums (e.g. Brighton and Hove Museum, 2005).The national museums were unable to return remains or indeed artefacts due to the terms of the Acts of Parliament under which they had been founded (e.g. the British Museum Act 1964 for the Natural History Museum, London). However, much of the debate was not predicated on this inability to return but on the scientific importance sometimes likening the return to book burning or religious suppression (e.g. BABAO, 2003; Brothwell, 2004). The scientific academic community did not think there would ever be the political will or that parliamentary time would be made to change the law to permit return.

This was to change in 2000 when the then UK Prime Minister, Tony Blair made an agreement with the then Australian Prime Minister John Howard to facilitate and promote the return of indigenous human remains to Australia (The Guardian, 2000). Initially people thought that this was the usual politicians' fine words. However, Tony Blair set up a working group to look into the whole issue of human remains in museums. The working group on human remains, under the chairmanship of Norman Palmer QC, began to take depositions from interested parties in 2001 and published its report in 2003 (DCMS, 2003). The panel had a cross-section of members from many different areas pertinent to the area; however, there was only a single scientist on the panel, the then Director of the Natural History Museum, Neil Chalmers, and no member had any direct experience of the care and conservation of or research using human remains. Although at the time this seemed to those constituting the panel a way of looking at the issues dispassionately, it was in fact a weakness of the working group. It meant that they came to it with their own prejudices of how museums held remains and had no one to provide a view of the reality. This would not have mattered so much had the working group been even-handed in the way it consulted with the different interest groups involved. Although many institutions were invited to submit evidence, the panel at no time visited museums or talked directly to researchers in the field (DCMS, 2003). They did, however, visit Australia to speak to indigenous groups and gauge their feelings. This left the scientific academic community feeling that they were not going to get a fair hearing and built up a degree of resentment before the report was even published (e.g. BABAO, 2003).

At the time, the report caused a furore. It had not looked at the actual behaviour of researchers and curators and made assumptions that caused outrage. Furthermore, it argued not only for a change in the law but for several other things, including a special panel, similar to the spoliation panel, to look at repatriation claims, and that museums should be proactive in finding the communities to which remains in their care belonged (DCMS, 2003). As was pointed out at the time in the minority report referred to below, to do so would paralyse the anthropology section of even a large museum, which would be able to do nothing but try to locate the groups affiliated to remains. They also argued for a licence system for holding human remains and for a full inventory of all remains in the United Kingdom to be undertaken. The costs involved would be prohibitive. This resulted in a minority report by the only scientist on the panel (DCMS, 2003).

Coincidentally, an Act of Parliament was being proposed to regulate the use of modern human tissue. This Act was in response to the Alder Hey and Bristol Children's Hospital scandals regarding tissue retained from babies and young children who had died from the 1980s onwards (BBC, 2001). This Act would include licensing for human remains less than 100 years old and gave the opportunity for the government to change the law to allow the national museums to de-accession human remains 1,000 years old or less (Human Tissue Act, 2004). This opened the way for the national museums, by far the largest holders of remains from former colonies, to consider requests for the return of remains to their country of origin.

The government department with responsibility for museums, the Department of Culture, Media and Sport, then set up a working group to consider the ways in which the Human Remains Working Group's recommendations could be implemented. The working group comprised a cross-section of those who worked in museums and other institutions and had responsibility for the care, curation and conservation of human remains as well as those who undertook research on human remains (DCMS, 2004). Once again a large number of institutions were invited to participate and the resulting document, the Guidance for the Care of Human Remains in Museums, is a workable and sensible one. It builds on existing best practice and also gives a framework for what needs to be considered when claims for the return of human remains are made (DCMS, 2004).

The changes in the law as outlined in the Human Tissue Act giving powers to de-accession to national museums came into force in 2006. During that first year alone agreements to return remains were made by British Museum, the Natural History Museum, the Liverpool Museums and the Science Museum.

7.3   Conclusions

Over the past decades in many countries there have been major changes in the way requests for return are considered. Countries such as the United States, United Kingdom and France have made changes to the law to allow returns to be made, a position unthinkable even twenty years ago – certainly during my career I have seen a major shift in attitude. There are still many in the academic community who find the return of remains anathema but changes in practice and the introduction of ethical codes by professional bodies such as the American Association of Physical Anthropologists (AAPA) and the British Association of Biological Anthropology and Osteoarchaeology (BABAO) are producing a new generation who regard access to human remains as a privilege not a right and take a more open approach to repatriation (Clegg, 2013b).

Questions

1 Did those who collected remains in the past know what they did was wrong?

Yes

No

2 Which of the following expressed a wish not to be placed in a museum?
A Truginini
B Ishi
C Pemuluy
D Pochatontas
E Charles Byrne

3 All attempts at repatriation have been for the benefit of the indigenous community concerned.
True
False

4 In the United States which was the first law allowing Native American remains to be returned?
A NMAIA
B NAGPRA
C HTA
D Cultural Property Act

5 NAGPRA covers more than ancestral remains?
True
False

6 In the United States which remains are illegal to trade in?
A All human remains
B Native American human remains
C Not illegal
D European remains

7 In Australia are the laws governing internal repatriation federal or state?
Federal
State

8 In New Zealand what constitutional document allows for the repatriation of Maori human remains?
A Treatment of Archaeological Remains Act
B Treaty of Waitanga

C No law exists

D Covered by international law

9 In the United Kingdom which Act of Parliament allowed the national museums to return human remains?

A British Museum Act

B Human Tissue Act

C Burial Act

D Ratification of the Hague Convention

8　Repatriation Today

The repatriation of human remains from indigenous communities held in museum collections has a history extending back over forty years (Fforde, 2004). Although communities in many countries have expressed interest in the return to country of origin of their ancestral human remains there are at present only three regions for which repatriation is a major international or national issue. These regions are Australia, New Zealand and North America, particularly the United States. It would be reasonable to assume that the driving forces behind repatriation were the same in all countries but this is not necessarily the case. There are similarities but national politics, local conditions and other factors have shaped the routes taken in each country, firstly for their national repatriation programmes and secondly for how international repatriations are organised and carried out. This chapter will examine the methods employed in each of these three countries and also outline the other countries that may in the future or are currently beginning to explore or undertake the return of remains from museums within their own country and internationally. In almost all European countries, with one exception, the repatriations are international. This is because in most countries museums transferred or otherwise obtained remains from around the world to ensure a global representation in their collections (Walker, 2000). It does now mean that countries actively seeking the return of remains on behalf of their own indigenous communities may also be asked for return by other countries. A good example here is the United States.

One issue that is consistent across the three countries which were early proponents of repatriation is that although, as in the United States (see below for more details), there was a movement for indigenous remains currently being excavated as part of rescue archaeology to be reburied, there was little push for remains in museums to be returned (Walker,

2000). The moving force behind the return from museums was, one might think unexpectedly, academics within the humanities and arts faculties who felt uncomfortable with their institution holding human remains from indigenous communities in their home country (Ousely et al., 2005). These academics made contact with community groups but for the most part the communities were more concerned by wider issues such as health care, and improving housing or educational opportunities for their community. In some cases the academics who felt their own sensibilities had been affronted by holding the remains lobbied their institutions for them to be returned (Lovell, 2007). Often they assumed that this would be what the community concerned would wish; however, in some cases this resulted in at best embarrassment for the community and at worst hostility from the community. For example, a Canadian institution returned remains to an Inuit community without contacting them first and without any consideration or research into cultural beliefs (Lovell, 2007). For many Inuit once a person dies their body is as nothing and is subject to taboos, but their spirit may return in a new-born to the tribe (Auger, 2005). The academics assumed they would be pleased by the return. However, while the community were very polite they were put in the embarrassing position of having to look after remains that culturally would never have been touched again (Auger, 2005), and for which they might now feel no connection.

Many communities that undertake repatriation say that they have had to overcome taboos to be able to undertake this work and actually view remains. Most Australian visitors are uncomfortable around the remains as the dead are often not mentioned again after death and grave sites are shunned for several years to allow the spirit to depart (Meehan, 1971). Any viewings of remains have to be handled carefully and sensitively, ensuring that it is the wish of the community and/or its representatives to actually see the remains, rather than a tick-box exercise to please the government department facilitating the request for return. That said, the remains can be valuable to the communities. Land claims often depend on showing a long relationship with a particular area. Being able to show that human remains dating to the time of European settlement of, for example, Australia were removed in the early colonial days helps to bolster these claims. There is also the issue of being able to pay their obligations to ancestors who are often viewed as part of life now and not, as a more western view would hold, as part of the past (Bin-Salik, 2007). This is to a large extent a healthy development which shows that, contrary to views expressed by some academics and politicians, Aboriginal culture is a living entity, not one set in stone. Any culture that wants to survive needs to be able to adapt to new situations and far from compromising their cultural heritage they are expressing this in new ways. The mismatch of assumptions between Western institutions and the communities is often at the root of problems in understanding each other's concerns.

8.1   The Emergence of Repatriation

There are, as presented in the previous chapter, common themes that have informed the emergence of repatriation within the different countries that currently actively make requests for return. These themes have centred on human rights and the treatment of human remains in the past through the treatment of individuals during colonial times or settlement by Europeans. The more recent treatment of remains both during excavations and in museums has highlighted the discrimination of indigenous peoples in their home country. If ancestral remains are not seen to be treated with respect this adds to the sense of injustice felt by communities when dealing with their own governments. The treatment of the dead as outlined in Chapter 4 shows that this can be seen as showing contempt for the conquered and has remained as such until very recently in the former colonial and European settled lands. The previous chapter highlighted examples of this and how the situation differs in places such as New Zealand compared to Australia and the United States.

Countries that pursue repatriation often begin with internal repatriation, giving back remains held in collections within the home country. Usually they progress to international requests when they have the backing of the home government or access to resources to undertake the discussions. Some countries undertake repatriation only as an international activity. Countries such as the United Kingdom do not have a minority indigenous population who are opposed but have to deal with the consequences of their colonial past.

8.2   The Current Position for Repatriation

More recently there has been a much wider acceptance that returning human remains to their country of origin is the right course of action. There is now more government commitment through both legislative changes and in fostering a more open approach. Curation and research staff within many of the major institutions that hold human remains are now more likely to support return of overseas or indigenous remains. This is often because older staff have retired or through dealing with repatriations have changed their views. Repatriations are now occurring from former colonial powers to African countries. Germany has recently returned the remains of people killed during an insurrection in Namibia in the early twentieth century. Their remains were taken to Germany and put in museums and included in research studies. In the past the view would have been that they should be kept (see Chapter 7), but today most people in European countries agree with the claimants that the remains should never have been taken in the first place. The return of remains is often seen today as restitution and so can help to heal past wrongs, both real and perceived.

Countries such as Australia and New Zealand have made more recent changes to their laws to further enhance the status of their indigenous human remains no matter what their age. For example, in New Zealand a recent statute by the New Zealand Government makes it a duty for all museums in the country that hold Maori remains to actively seek their return to the community.

8.3   Case Study in Repatriation

It is often instructive to look at the consequences of how repatriation is handled. This is more telling when the claimant communities are not resident in the country whose institutions hold these overseas remains. This is not only true for former colonial powers but also for current claimant countries which will hold within their legacy collections remains that were collected, traded or swapped with other institutions. The situation is different from that when dealing with people in the same country and it is often harder to understand the drivers for requests, at least at first.

The Natural History Museum, London

The NHM had been one of the most vociferous of the museums in its opposition to repatriation (Chalmers, 2003; Stringer, 2003). The general feeling was that returning even the small percentage of the total collection of human remains, which is in excess of 25,000 individuals, with between 10 and 20 per cent from former, would be the beginning of the breaking up of a great national collection and potentially the end of research using human remains. To this end all arguments presented by museum staff concentrated on the importance of the collection to science (Deposition to Human Remains Working Group, DCMS, 2003). However, this was often presented in a vague and nebulous manner with few examples of how research on remains benefited modern populations but rather focusing on the broader picture of how research was useful. Interestingly, although in fact talking about research on the whole collection, the case presented rarely stated this and so gave the impression that the research was carried out purely on remains from overseas indigenous communities. The communities that came to the museum were equally blinkered and were more likely to taunt the scientists about putting remains out of the reach of science once they got them back. This of course did nothing for relationships, resulting in what can only be described as a dialogue of the deaf, with everyone speaking but no one listening – which is of course a prerequisite for a conversation and mutual understanding.

In 2006 the museum, because of the change in the law, had to consider claims for return. It implemented a system of checking the provenance of the remains mostly through archival research and a basic physical examination of the remains. The work was undertaken by a newly appointed member of staff for whom this was the sole responsibility. To ensure impartiality, the museum set up a human remains advisory panel to consider the evidence presented by both the museum staff and by the community making the claim. In common with the government working party, this advisory panel had no members who undertook research on human remains. This was a fatal flaw in the process and ultimately cost the museum dear.

The first claim to be considered was from the Australian Government and the Tasmanian Aboriginal Council (TAC). In retrospect this was not the ideal claim to be dealt with first but the Australian Government seemed to have a policy of dealing with the people who shouted loudest. The TAC representatives had on previous visits to the museum expressed the view that they would destroy the remains should they be returned to them so that they could no longer be available for research – in their words, 'put them beyond the reach of science'. The Tasmanian remains were of particular scientific importance as the number of remains worldwide was small and the Tasmanians had possibly been isolated for anything up to 10,000 years before the Europeans arrived in Australia. The remains had been used extensively in research in the previous ten years and had even been part of an early worldwide DNA study.

The report from the museum staff suggested that the remains were too valuable to science to be returned, while the TAC argued that they should be returned to allow the spirit of the ancestors to rest. This was actually no change in the views of either side. The advisory panel recommended a course of action that pleased neither side: the remains should be returned but a period of study should be allowed to permit the newer techniques that might be used in the future to be applied to the remains. The TAC objected but the NHM Trustees decided to implement this decision.

The study period began and all the non-invasive work such as measurements, scanning, casting and detailed observations were made. The next step would have been to take samples for DNA and isotope analysis and to section some teeth for microscopic analysis. The TAC applied to a Tasmanian court to be made executors or administrators of the estates of these long-dead people, with the help of the Australian barrister Geoffrey Robertson, who practised in London. The members of the TAC were appointed administrators and using this power they applied to the High Court in London for an injunction to stop all analysis using the remains. The case should have been heard quite quickly but many other parties became involved or expressed interest. A huge amount of paperwork was generated and the previous DNA study was disclosed as the lab involved was to have undertaken the additional DNA analysis. The judge suggested that the NHM and TAC try mediation. The process was set up and over three days agreement was reached that all the non-invasive work would be completed and that DNA from the original study should be held in joint custody by the TAC and NHM. The TAC also agreed not to destroy the remains but to rebury them.

The court case and mediation are often misquoted and presented as if the NHM was not going to return the remains. That was never the case; the Tasmanian remains were to be returned as soon as the study period was complete. The case raises several issues. The first was that the study was only recommended because the TAC representatives had said on several occasions that they intended to destroy the remains to put them beyond the reach of science. The NHM as a scientific institution felt that the scientific value had to be retained because the remains would be destroyed. In retrospect, had the TAC representatives said nothing then the whole issue may not have arisen. It also became obvious during the mediation process that there was a serious misunderstanding about what the various techniques did and what destructive testing actually involved. When NHM staff had the opportunity, after the mediation process was complete, to show the TAC representatives what happened and what was involved the representatives were extremely surprised at how minimal the damage to the remains was. It seemed that the advice they had received was many years out of date and did not represent the current situation for molecular analysis. However, even a better understanding of the processes involved in molecular analysis might not have prevented the court case, as many Australian Aboriginal people, and especially those from Tasmania, were worried that DNA analysis would be used to determine whether they were of Aboriginal descent.

The whole process involved in this first claim for return made the museum re-evaluate what and how to approach this matter. The review came up with several suggestions for improving the situation. The first was to set up a separate unit, the Human Remains Unit, to tackle all the issues surrounding human remains. The major part of the unit's work would be repatriation but the unit staff would also deal with all Human Tissue Act matters, take decisions about access to remains, including destructive testing, give advice on exhibiting remains and undertake not only to improve the provenance of remains under claim for return but to expand this to the whole modern human collection.

Repatriation claims would also be handled differently to the original methods used for the Tasmanian claim. The provenance would, as before, involve a full archival research project but the physical examination would be based on that undertaken by the National Museum of Natural History at the Smithsonian Institute before remains are returned to Native American Nations. Furthermore, there would be engagement with the claimant on the value of science and human remains, on other related issues and a greater sharing of the information the provenancing produced.

The next claim gave the NHM an opportunity to try out this new method. This was the request for the Torres Strait Island (TSI) human

Figure 8.1 Meeting with TSI representatives on Mabauig 2009.
© The Trustees of the Natural History Museum London

remains, made by the Torres Strait Traditional Owners and the Australian Government. It was a very large claim and would take a considerable amount of time to complete (Clegg & Long, 2015). This gave ample opportunity to meet with the community. In 2009 museum staff, including the Head of the Human Remains Unit (HRU) and the relevant Keeper, had the opportunity to visit Australia to present this new approach at an anthropology conference. While in Australia the Head of the HRU and the Keeper arranged to visit the Torres Strait Islands (Figure 8.1). By coincidence a consultation was being undertaken about what the islanders would like to have happen should more remains be returned (including those from the NHM). The NHM staff visiting Australia were fortunate to attend some of these meetings and hear the islanders' views, of the ordinary islanders not just of community leaders. It also gave the two staff members the opportunity to forge closer links with the Community Elders and take every opportunity to explain what was done to the remains and why and what this information could tell us all. Some concrete examples of studies that had impacted on modern people were also included and it became obvious that the community were very interested in this and that there was still the lingering suspicion that work on human remains was limited to those from indigenous communities.

Over the next two years visits were arranged both in London and by museum staff to the islands. This culminated in the NHM trustees agreeing to return remains unconditionally and offering a fellowship to a young Torres Strait Islander to learn about the museum's work in this field and for the islander to share traditional knowledge about remains with museum staff.

The department of the Australian Government that deals with repatriation was so taken with this idea of a fellowship that it also funded a fellowship for a mainland native Australian to be included. The posts were advertised and over ninety people applied. The choice was very difficult because the calibre of the applicants was so high, but eventually two people were chosen. They took up their positions in October 2011. It was a hard adjustment for both fellowship holders but they took on the challenge and worked hard both to assimilate and to disseminate a huge amount of information. The same was true for museum staff, as information from the two fellowship holders often challenged existing beliefs and assumptions.

The return of a number of the remains of Torres Strait people was scheduled for November of that year (Figure 8.2). The advice from both fellowship holders to the Human Remains Unit, but particularly from our Torres Strait colleague, made the return an amazing success. The whole process had built such a good relationship that it was much easier to discuss difficult issues.

One of these was the problem of a large number of remains taken from a sacred cave on Pulu off the coast of Mabauig in the strait. These remains were trophy heads and although the provenance showed that the remains had been collected from the cave, the nature of their original collection meant that it was not possible to determine which island they actually originated from or even if they were from Papua New Guinea (PNG) rather than the Torres Strait. The trade in heads is discussed in detail in Chapter 1. There had been a widespread trade across the strait from PNG and so the remains could have been Papuan (Haddon, 1904). The islanders were keen to know the place of origin for these remains. All archival and

Figure 8.2 Torres Strait human remains being loaded for their journey home.
© The Trustees of the Natural History Museum London

non-invasive methods had been exhausted, which left only molecular analysis to shed light on the matter. The islanders suggested that the remains be left at the NHM until such time as they decided the exact methods they would want to be used and that they would work with NHM staff to undertake this work.

The fellowships have also been successful with other communities, although at present the NHM needs to find new sources of funding for future fellowships. However, that the NHM has undertaken one such venture and hopes to do so again has shown the will to take plans forward and a commitment to offering educational opportunities to indigenous people. The fellowships have also given the NHM new contacts for any return to the Northern Territory. As part of the fellowships the two fellowship holders gave presentations to other groups and at museums across Australia. This has helped to develop the NHM's profile in Australia. In addition, both museum staff and the fellowship holders have presented in other areas outside the United Kingdom and Australia and the NHM's new approach has now been widely discussed and is appreciated by many communities and museums. The HRU also gave advice to other museums on how to set up a similar type of process or to provenance human remains for smaller institutions and the Australian Government has found this helpful in their dealings with museums in the United Kingdom and in Europe.

8.4 Other International Repatriations

There is now acceptance in the United States, Europe, Australia and other countries that remains they hold that originate from outside their own borders should be considered for return. The United States has found this particularly difficult, for several reasons. At present they are still deeply involved in their own internal repatriations, and there is no commitment or legislation that requires them to return overseas remains. This means that unlike returns under the NAGPRA there is no funding for the type of work that needs to be undertaken to ensure that remains originate in the claimant country or that they are affiliated to the claimant group. However, this is the same position as most European countries, including the United Kingdom, which have no additional government funding available to undertake the necessary work but that has not prevented this work occurring.

Many of the African countries are now expressing interest in repatriation of remains removed during their colonial period. One country for which this has been successful is Namibia regarding remains removed during this country's colonial occupation by Germany (BBC News, 2011). During Germany's colonial occupation there were massacres of Namibian nationals. The bodies of these people were removed, rendered into skeletal remains and taken to Germany for both research and display. The Namibian Government asked that the German institutions return these remains, which they did during 2013. Given the success of this return it is likely that more countries will contact the various European countries that held territory in Africa during the nineteenth and twentieth centuries.

There has been much progress in the area of repatriation, with many European countries now taking this issue seriously and putting matters in hand to facilitate the return of remains to their country of origin. This has meant in some cases, such as in the United Kingdom or in France, that the law has to be changed to allow such returns to occur. The legal aspects of human remains in general and of repatriation in particular was addressed in Chapter 3 devoted to legal aspects of human remains.

Questions

1 Why do museums worldwide have indigenous remains from other countries?

2 How were some early repatriations handled?
A Very well
B Poorly
C None until laws were passed

3 What is the major stumbling block to remains being returned even when there is a will to return?
A Cost
B Lack of communication
C No records of where remains are from
D No requests for return

4 What was the most usual defence for not returning remains?
A Against the law
B Scientific value of remains
C Cost of return
D No will to return

5 What was the real reason NHM could not consider claims for return?
A Scientific value of remains
B Costs of return
C Not enough staff
D British Museum Act prohibited return

6 How did the return to TSI differ from that to Tasmania?

7 What benefits did the fellowships bring to the NHM?
   A Goodwill
   B Collaboration
   C Contacts in other communities
   D All of the above

8 Why are international returns in the United States problematic?

9 Countries from which regions are now taking an interest in repatriation?
   A Asia
   B Africa
   C Indian subcontinent
   D Pacific islands

10 Which two European countries have changed their laws to allow human remains to be returned?
   A Germany
   B Spain
   C France
   D Italy

9   The Importance of Provenance

The provenance of human remains is crucial to the understanding of the origin of remains held within museum collections. This is vital not only for the return of remains to their country of origin but to inform and enhance the relevance of remains for research. It is generally assumed that all items in museum collections are fully documented and all relevant information recorded (Clegg, 2009). This is the case for items accessioned by museums today; there are agreed standards for the information to be recorded and legal and ethical requirements, including legislation, to ensure that items in museums are held legally. This has sadly not always been so. Until the last thirty years there were no agreed standards within institutions and no consistency between institutions (Redfern & Bekvalac, 2013). The information recorded seemingly depended on the whim of the curator entering the information, the amount of material to be recorded on a given day or over a time period and how important the curator thought the item was to the museum (Clegg, 2009). An additional issue can occur with the documentation of human remains: the obscuring, either intentionally or not, of the full origin of the remains. This was not so prevalent during the nineteenth or even the early twentieth century but increased from the middle of the twentieth century, as people became more aware of the true nature and impact of some collecting, especially for remains from colonial countries. This means it is often difficult to be certain that the basic record within the museum database gives the full information about the remains. The task of bringing old museum records to modern standards is often time-consuming but without accurate information the remains are of less scientific value than those with good provenance. The checking of information that is often undertaken as part of any process of returning the remains usually improves the provenance, which ensures that remains are returned at least to the right region. This also enhances their importance as a research resource (Ousely et al., 2005).

9.1   How to Provenance Human Remains

The provenance of remains can be determined in two ways: the archival information relating to the remains and information from the bones themselves (Clegg, 2009). When used together these two methods can extract the maximum amount of information and ensure that the archive information is not used in isolation. At a minimum, the remains should be checked against the original information from the donor or the earliest record of the remains at the institution. This ensures that what is found in the box is what's described in the records. There are many cases where these records don't match and reasons for the mismatch then need to be investigated. The complete information about any donation may actually be held by the institution but may be separated from the original basic record which was derived from this source; for example, the original donation letter is often not with the general record but may be in the institution's archive.

Archival Research

The simplest form of archival research is that for remains which were direct donations to the institution as this generally means that most of the information is likely to be held at the home institution. In more complex cases, when remains have been held at one or more institutions or within other collections, the simplest method is still to check within the holding institutions to ensure that all information supplied on transfer is recorded in the main record for each individual and that the two sets of information tally in respect of the skeletal elements present.

This would generally be sufficient if the records were merely being updating to ensure that all information held is recorded to modern standards. However, when undertaking repatriation, especially for remains that have passed through many different collections, it is important that these sources are also checked, especially for remains long held in the previous collection(s), where information is more likely not to have been transferred. Indeed, it is rare for archive information to be transferred with remains as this is seen as part of the archive of the institution rather than of the specimen. This process is time-consuming, yet the embarrassment of returning remains to the wrong country holds a greater cost in both reputational damage and loss of trust for an institution. One institution returned remains to Tasmania without undertaking any checks other than that the box holding the remains was listed on the index card in the institution's files. At a later date Te Papa Museum's repatriation unit undertook its own research into remains removed from New Zealand by a particular individual and found that some of the remains returned to Tasmania were in fact from New Zealand. This necessitated protracted negotiations between the Tasmanian Aboriginal Council (TAC) and Te Papa to return the remains to New Zealand (Clegg, 2009). A simple check through the institution's archives would have prevented this situation.

If a full archival research project is undertaken either as part of the process of return or to fully update the records then the project needs to be properly planned and not conducted in an ad hoc fashion. Several institutions have begun such projects, including the Smithsonian's Natural History Museum in Washington, the Natural History Museum in London and Adelaide Museum in Australia. These projects are likely to take many years as the remains held in these institutions often have complicated histories or involve large numbers of remains. They are not only in order to facilitate repatriation but also to update and improve knowledge of collections to be retained, making them more useful for research. Other institutions, such as the Museum of London, have collected more complete data for many years. However, in the case of the Museum of London all the remains are from archaeological contexts and from the London area. The methods used by all of these institutions is very similar; all use best practice and often discuss working methods to ensure that the data collected is compatible and in similar formats to allow information to be more easily shared. Data compatibility means that, for example, when remains from the same donor were given to different institutions then the information about them is more easily passed between institutions in a readily usable form. The methods used by the institutions discussed above are now also being implemented by many other museums when such projects are initiated.

Once a full archival research project is conceived, the institution concerned needs to undertake careful planning of the information to be collected and what depth of information will be collected. These projects are, as mentioned earlier, time-consuming but with good planning and by looking at the methods used elsewhere they can be fairly straightforward.

The information already available for the whole or part of the collection to be provenanced needs to be checked for accuracy. This is best done through an audit of the remains within the store, initially checking that the listing of elements in the records matches those held in each box. Any dates in the records, usually registers and index cards, should be checked against any information on the box or the remains themselves. It is often worthwhile using ultraviolet light to check for anything written on the bones that might have disappeared or faded over time.

Once all the information readily available has been assembled then any additional information needed should be assessed. The information most often available is the general place of collection, the donor's and/or collector's name, the date of donation, whether remains were transferred from another collection and a list of the skeletal elements present both currently and when donated. From this information an assessment can be made of whether any more information can be gathered. If it seems possible to collect more information then the next step is to identify the archives in which any relevant information may be held. These might be in other institutions, if the remains were previously held in other collections; the archives associated with the donor, which can be personal archives if they are important or famous people; or the archives of any institution or organisation associated with the donor or collector. For example, information about doctors or surgeons can often be found in medical association records, or more general sources of information can be used; these might be newspaper reports from the time, national archives, which hold items such as ship's manifests, or official reports.

Once sufficient information is collected to complete a chain from collection to acceptance into the current collection, the information can be collated for each individual ensuring that they are, at least from documentary sources, shown to have been collected as described. Of course, in anything up to 20 per cent of cases this process will show that the remains are not as described in the original records but that some change has been made through mis-transcription (Figure 9.1), error or deliberately, sometimes to enhance the value of remains sold to institutions in earlier times (Clegg, 2009).

The most difficult remains to deal with are those bought at auction. It is rare to be able to trace these to the exact sale and even when this is possible it is even rarer, in my own experience impossible, to find any documentary

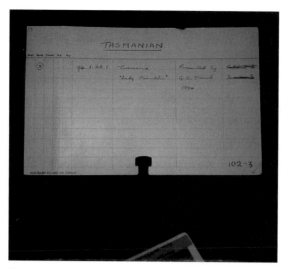

Figure 9.1 Example of a transcription error for NHM Tasmanian remains.
© The Trustees of the Natural History Museum London

evidence linking remains to their country of origin. The information is purely that given to the auctioneer by the seller. Many sellers do not know the true origin of the remains or, if professional collectors who sell for profit, they will sometimes change the origin to that which is most 'fashionable' at the time. Particularly in earlier times the auction house would have listed the remains as described by the seller and would hold no further information, even if such records survive. This is where deliberate changes often occur. If the provenance has been as part of a process of return then this information should be shared with the claimant community or nation. Generally, once there is full information showing that remains aren't as they have been described, when claimants accept this they will all say they only want their own people home. Where the documentation process is to bring the record-keeping up to modern standards then the curation staff can use them to better inform visiting researchers as to the true origin of the remains in their care.

Physical Examination

The extent to which a physical examination of remains should be undertaken will depend on the time and resources available to permit this.

However, although time-consuming it is best not to rely completely on the archival evidence when provenancing remains. At the simplest level the boxes should be opened, the elements present should be checked and a simple assessment of age and sex should be made. This ensures that at a minimum the information held in the individual remains record as to number and type of bones and the age and sex has been verified (Clegg, 2009).

As part of any repatriation process most institutions undertake this simple checking process. Many institutions, including the Smithsonian's Natural History Museum, the Natural History Museum in London and the National Museum of Natural History in New York, undertake far greater physical examinations. These include examination for activity, disease and trauma that might be consistent with a particular region or group, examination of the shape of the skull using standard measurements, which are then compared to a forensic database of such measurements such as FORDISC or CRANID (Figure 9.2).

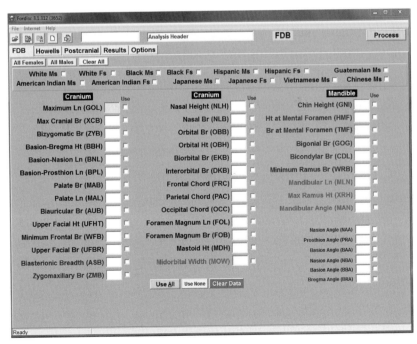

Figure 9.2 Input screen for FORDISC measurements.
© The Trustees of the Natural History Museum London

In 1990 a set of standards specifically for use with remains for return was developed at a workshop in the United States. These standards were published as Standards for Examination of the Human Skeleton by Buikstra and Ubalaker (1994). This is the best and most complete manual available, although it was really developed for Native American remains and slight changes may need to be made when looking at remains from elsewhere in the world. This is especially so for dental traits but other areas too may need modifying. However, if used in conjunction with known information for the relevant ethnic or geographic group then consistency between institutions can be maintained. The standards are truly comprehensive and if all were used then the time involved would be immense. It is best to take the most general, such as age, sex, trauma and pathologies, and then use ethnographically appropriate methods, such as checking activity against the ethnographic or other contemporary literature to understand lifestyles (Clegg, 2009).

Other Methods to Assist with Provenance

There are other methods, techniques and resources that can be used to improve provenance. Historic records and resources not directly related to the remains or the donor/collector can put the remains in context, particularly if they are archaeological or even historic. Examining the ethnographic record for the region in question is helpful in putting together a picture of the area as it was traditionally. Modern techniques such as DNA and isotope analysis can also be used. These need caution particularly for indigenous remains, as many groups are opposed to such testing. There are, in addition, ethical issues in the use particularly of DNA analysis, especially if the remains have identifiable descendants (Redfern & Clegg, 2017). The results may show inherited diseases and such information needs careful handling by experts in DNA counselling.

Ethnography

Undertaking an ethnographic study of the country or group in question can assist in understanding what is seen in both the physical examination and the archival research. The remains being examined may be relatively recent, from places such as former colonies or newly settled lands, or they may be historic or archaeological. For the relatively modern remains it is possible to get a picture of people's lives at the time of first contact. Many books were written at the time about the people of other countries, and this is particularly true for former colonies of countries such as Britain or France or within newly formed states such as the United States or Canada. These give the reader a view, albeit often biased, of the activities and customs of the people in the region. Customs surrounding death are often given and this can help when identifying obvious post mortem trauma or other evidence such as tooth loss. It can also assist by ruling out some individuals as being part of any group: for example, if tooth ablation is not routinely part of the mourning ritual or any initiation ceremony then tooth loss is likely to be from another cause.

However, if a whole group have similar tooth loss and the ethnographic literature shows such activity was part of a life stage then they are more likely to be from that group. The ethnographic literature encompasses not only accounts written at the time but also more recent analysis using both archaeological and contemporary accounts. These sources might include postgraduate theses. I have used several of these and they are good for identifying rare resources that only someone undertaking such detailed research would find. One example is Meehan's thesis on mortuary rites in Australian aboriginal people which not only brings together the differences in practice across Australia but also gives difficult-to-find references.

Historical and Other Resources

Historic resources can be extremely helpful for both recent and ancient remains. In a similar way to the ethnographic record they are accounts which either draw on ancient sources, in the case of the long dead, or draw together records from the times for which there are written records, such as the Roman Empire or medieval Europe. It is also helpful to look at information found on the bones through the lens of past people. Something that has left a mark on the bones may be difficult to explain or use in provenance but if accounts of people who live in similar environments or undertook similar activities are included then, for example, trauma patterns can be more easily explained. Interestingly this was recently undertaken for Neanderthal remains in which a particular pattern of fractures was found. The research team looked at many different groups and found that the one with the most similar pattern were rodeo riders, who are work closely with large mammals. This indicated that the Neanderthals too were very close to their prey when hunting (Berger & Trinkaus, 1995).

Modern Techniques

The bones themselves can give more information since it became possible to extract DNA from ancient bones and to analyse the composition of the isotopes. These techniques are improving all the time and perhaps one day we may not even need to take a sample. It is now possible to soak insect specimens in a special solution into which their DNA leeches and can then be analysed without destroying any part of the specimen. These newer techniques are among those used in forensic analysis to help determine an unknown deceased person's identity and for this reason are sometimes acceptable to indigenous communities.

aDNA

This technique is a valuable method for testing information about the remains. However, there are drawbacks. Since there is not yet a fully comprehensive database showing ancestry, many regions of the world have limited or no data available with which to compare the results. Furthermore, modern migration has changed the genetic composition in many regions, which will mean that current populations may not be the same genetically as they were in the past, even though they may be direct descendants. This is also true where there has been colonisation and long-term trading with other areas. It has been suggested that ancestry sites might help but as they are compiled using modern data they suffer from all of the problems detailed above. However, the data can give personal information and can be compared to DNA from living descendants, if they agree. This does need caution, and the involvement of researchers trained in the implications of using DNA from living people is necessary. The analysis may show information which is not known to the present-day descendants. There may – and this will become increasing common as more markers are found for diseases – be information of a sensitive nature that could have a radical impact. It is therefore important that before undertaking such analyses the curator considers these ethical issues and takes advice from independent experts or an ethics panel. This issue is discussed in more depth in papers such as Redfern and Clegg (2017).

DNA analysis is controversial when used in repatriation contexts. Many indigenous groups, particularly in the recent past, have been very much against its use. Indeed several institutions have been taken to court to try to prevent such analysis occurring. The Natural History Museum in London was challenged in the courts by the Tasmanian Aboriginal Council in 2007 when its researchers tried to undertake molecular analysis on remains due to be returned (see Chapter 8 for a full discussion). However, times are changing and, provided communities are consulted and involved, some groups are now willing to discuss such analyses and some have used it for provenancing.

Isotope Analysis

This technique can be used to determine several factors which have implications for estimating the location of an individual. We are what we eat. This is important as what we eat and drink become part of our bodies and so leave an indelible mark within us that can be used to show where we grew up, where we lived for the last few years and the sort of food in our diet, which can also show the region we live in. This is true whether we are alive or dead.

Our teeth are a record of what happened when they formed. All our teeth, including our permanent dentition, form during our childhood so our teeth are a time capsule of that part of our lives. Teeth are not remodelled, as are bones, during our lifetimes and so they can give a large amount of information about what was happening as they formed (Hillson, 1996). The water we drink passes through rock and picks up different isotopes depending on the chemical composition of the rock. This can be used to show the most likely place where a person grew up. The technique is used in forensic science when unknown individuals are found and there is no other means of identifying them (Dikmaat, 2015). This technique has the potential to aid in deciding where the person whose skeleton or skull is being claimed for return grew up. This can not only show that they, for example, grew up in Australia but also helps narrow down the area of Australia.

Our bones, on the other hand, remodel over about a ten-year period so only the last few years of our lives are recorded (White *et al.*, 2012). However, from our bones we can look at the type of diet eaten and compare this with the food sources found in a region to see whether, for example, more terrestrial animals have been eaten compared to either freshwater or marine fish. The vegetable matter eaten also has its own signature and depending on whether it is for example C_3 (such as wheat, rice, barley and oats) or C_4 (such as maize and millet), plants can show where the individual has lived for the past few years of their life. In some respects this is more useful for people from the past as today it is not unusual for people to eat foods imported from many countries and therefore eat food from regions where they do not live. However, many skeletal remains likely to be claimed for repatriation are from a time when this would have been uncommon. Therefore the technique can pinpoint more exactly the likely place of origin, although those who lived on, for example, mission stations may not show local signatures as their diet will have been more like the colonisers' and contain foods not native to the region. However, this change in diet, if found in a collection of remains, can help confirm archival information or pinpoint possible dates for collection. Recently, analysis of skeletal remains from South Australia had the dietary information as supplied by isotope analysis used to determine which region of South Australia each individual came from. This was because some groups in this part of Australia eat freshwater fish, some eat marine fish and others only eat terrestrial animals. It would have been impossible to decide which community should have which individuals returned to them without this analysis (Pate *et al.*, 2002). The skeletal remains, although provenanced to South Australia by other methods, could not have been differentiated otherwise.

Using Methods for Provenance

It is important when provenancing human remains that the most appropriate techniques are used. This ensures that information relevant to both the remains and their likely geographic grouping are collected to ensure that resources are not wasted and that the work proceeds in a timely fashion. When remains are claimed for return it is even more important than for routine collections to undertake a provenance exercise as it is essential that both the community and the decision makers, such as museum trustees, have full confidence that the remains are being returned to the correct people. Most communities frequently say that they only want their own people to come home (e.g. David, pers. comm.), and using the methods described can only increase confidence that this is so. However, all parties should be aware of the process involved in provenancing, which is why a clear policy and procedures for repatriation is so important. If all parties are fully informed at the outset then misunderstandings are less likely to occur. The community requesting the remains should be kept updated on information discovered during the repatriation process and copies of both the final report and the data for each individual should be shared.

The amount of work that can be done does depend on the monies available but some form of provenance should be undertaken at least to ensure that the records and the remains match – that they are indeed what it says on the box. If more detailed work such as destructive or transformative analysis is to be included in any provenance then the community should be consulted. The implications discussed and the likelihood of success must be high before any such analysis is performed. The fears of communities regarding destructive and transformative analysis was discussed earlier and it is essential that they feel comfortable with these techniques being carried out. It may mean that the remains are not as well provenanced as they could be but these tests can be conducted at a later stage when communities feel more comfortable with them. There is more widespread knowledge of these techniques in a forensic setting, popularised through shows such as *CSI*, *Bones* and *NCIS*. However, this can lead to unrealistic expectations as there is no problem of funding or other issues in such shows. While it does make discussing such methods easier, as with the early repatriations any return should be about the feelings of the community not the feelings of the people returning remains.

9.2   Conclusions

Provenance is a vital part of understanding collections of human remains held in museums. The minimum should be that basic records and the remains in each box are checked to ensure that they are what is claimed. When remains are claimed for return this is essential. Institutions normally undertake comprehensive provenance exercises for remains likely to be returned to either the claimant community or the country of origin. However, when funds permit this is also good practice for all collections retrospectively. Best practice should be used to ensure that recently acquired human remains have a full set of information to ensure good documentation and to enable the best possible use for research. Molecular techniques should be used ethically and with regard to the wishes of descendant communities. It is also essential that all information discovered during the repatriation process is shared with the communities.

Questions

1 Why might museum staff in the past have not fully recorded details of remains in their collections?

A To hide origin of the remains

B Not had time to record all information

C Information not given by donor

D Didn't think it was important

E No agreed standards

2 What errors can be found in museum documents?

A Transcription

B Omissions

C Changes

D All of the above

3 What is the first task to undertake when provenancing human remains?

A Take measurements

B Archival research

C Check remains in the box match records

D Take samples for analysis

4 Should more or less archival research be undertaken for remains to be repatriated?
More
Less

5 Select three institutions that have or are undertaking provenancing of their human remains.
A Smithsonian
B Natural History Museum, London
C Natural History Museum, New York
D Adelaide Museum

6 Why is it important for museums to standardise the information they collect or record?

7 What is the minimum physical examination of human remains that should take place?
A CRANID or FORDISK analysis
B Check the remains against the museum records
C Check age and sex of remains
D All of the above

8 Which of the following can aid in provenancing?
A Archival research
B Physical examination
C Ethnography
D All of the above

9 Select two modern techniques that have been used to aid in provenancing.
A Scanning
B DNA analysis
C Isotope analysis
D Analysis of dental calculus

10 How does improved provenance aid scientific research?

10   Reburial and the Alternatives

Reburial is often thought of as primarily involving human remains from indigenous communities. While this aspect of reburial of human remains is the one that is most often reported it is not the only case in which human remains might be reburied. In many European museums only a relatively small number of remains are from former colonies. The majority of remains, particularly those disinterred through archaeological excavations, are from the country in which the museum is situated. These remains are often kept in museums but their fate is decided by either legal requirements or other considerations.

10.1   Reburial and Archaeological Human Remains

When human remains are excavated as part of archaeological investigations it is usual in most European countries to give consideration to the eventual fate of these remains. It is widely assumed that all such remains will be deposited in museum collections. This may have been true in the past but today, although human remains are studied to give a greater understanding of life in the past, it is not necessarily the case that they will be permanently kept in a museum or other institution. Sometimes remains will be reburied either after initial documentation or within a few years of excavation. This will depend on a variety of factors, such as the age of the remains – with more recent remains more likely to be reburied – and the state of the remains – those in a poor state which might cause health issues for the living are usually reburied or cremated immediately. Space within museum collections is another factor; many museums have limited ability to accept large numbers of remains and so short-term storage and study may be more appropriate if remains are not of great scientific interest. The feelings of the local community or any genetic descendants may also be important in reaching the decision on whether to rebury or not. At present in the United Kingdom this is decided on a case-by-case basis.

10.2   Reburial and Ancient Remains

Within museum collections there are often large numbers of human remains from civilisations or cultures that no longer exist because of the time that has elapsed. We often have limited knowledge of their culture and try to glean this from both the artefacts and the remains they leave behind. Requests to rebury such remains often come from special interest groups such as the Pagans and Druids in the United Kingdom and Europe. They often ask that remains are given to them and reburied in their own version of the ancient culture. One problem with such reburials is that, given the size of past populations, these ancient remains will be the ancestors of many modern people alive today. Pagans and Druids often ask for remains that are outside of the scope of the Human Tissue Act and the Guidance on Human Remains (DCMS, 2004), so legally there are sometimes problems with allowing such requests. However, given that such remains are often the ancestors of many present-day Europeans it is not equitable to acquiesce to a single group's request. In the United Kingdom, in common with many European countries, the public, many of whom are descended from these remains, expect to see human remains held in museums and are comfortable with them being included in scientific studies. Indeed, a survey showed that even when people wanted the remains to be reburied many only wanted this to occur after the remains had been studied (Historic England, 2009).

10.3   Reburial and Repatriation

The expected result from the repatriation of human remains to their country of origin is reburial or, in a proportion of cases, burial of the remains (see Chapter 8 for further discussion). Indigenous communities feel the need to complete the burial process and associated mortuary rituals that their ancestors would have undergone at the time of their death. In some cases the remains will never have been buried and may not have been subject to any traditional mortuary rituals. It is often not clear from the records held in museums, even after extensive archival research, whether burial had taken place. When records do exist they may show burial as complete or that traditional rituals were interrupted. This later is often the case when bodies were removed from places used to expose remains after death, such as trees or specially constructed platforms. Communities also want to treat the remains with dignity and respect, often viewing burial/ reburial as part of this process. Furthermore, the interruption of mortuary rituals is viewed as interfering with the movement of the deceased person's spirit to the next stage towards rebirth (see Chapter 8 for further details).

The burial process can be a distressing event for the community and can cause much discussion and sometimes disagreement as to exactly how it should proceed. There is also the issue of costs. Some governments, such as Australia, provide funds very readily to bring the remains home. However, the monies for reburial are often not part of this funding and communities have to either apply to a different funding stream or raise the funds themselves. It can therefore be a long-drawn-out process (see later in this chapter for further discussion of the issue), and leave a community feeling distressed and troubled.

In the early days of repatriation, reburial or even cremation was seen as a way of fully regaining control over the fate of the remains of these long-dead people. It was also seen as stopping scientists, who had not always been respectful of others' beliefs, from gaining access to the remains. It is sometimes viewed by communities as an affirmation of traditional beliefs and culture which can draw together all parts of the community to rebuild a feeling of autonomy and dignity.

10.4   Alternatives to Reburial

Despite the assumption that reburial is synonymous with repatriation, this is not necessarily the case. One of the major issues often raised during discussions regarding the return of remains either to country of origin or to the group most culturally or genetically related to the remains is one of control over the remains. This generally means that the community wants to decide who gets access, what happens to the remains and under what circumstances. In reality this is often one of the major concerns of groups and communities that ask for remains to be returned to them. It is the feeling of these groups that things are done to them and their ancestors without permission. This has been a constant theme in all discussions about repatriation. This is why reburial often takes place in the early days of repatriation. It was the driving force for example in the United States for the reburial of remains after excavations (Fine-Dare, 2002). The idea that others can decide about ancestral remains that have no connection to them was always a major issue for indigenous communities.

There are several ways of addressing such concerns, the main being to fully engage with communities and begin to understand how important this is to them. It is an ethical issue, and the points presented in Chapter 4, such as raiding graveyards and ignoring the express wishes of the person whose bones are taken for a museum, are ones which must be considered. The First Nations of many countries have had things done to them and their ancestors which we would not countenance now. We need to take an ethical stance on these issues and use it to aid in understanding why people feel as they do.

We should try to bring about a greater understanding of the importance of research using human remains to both the community concerned and to the wider community. Interestingly, the preponderance of TV shows such as *CSI* and *NCIS* have brought forensic work to the fore, which has had a positive effect on how research into human remains is now perceived. Even the resistance to physical examination of the remains seems to disappear when couched in the right terms, as giving back the identity of the person whose remains have been anonymous for so long. This is even more evident when the institution holding the remains shows that they will share all information discovered through the work undertaken and that any other access to this information would only be allowed with the consent of the claimant community. Even though it is rare to be able to put a name to the person, the information collected does allow appropriate treatment in accordance with, for example, age and sex that is used by a specific community. This is essentially by returning the humanity to the bones in collections and treating them as one would any other person whose identity has been lost and which we wish to restore.

For some communities the most important aspect of a return is that the remains are held on 'home territory' and that, depending on local tradition, this may be sufficient either to bring peace to the person or to heal old injustices, as well as providing restitution to the community (Fforde, 2004). Some communities are working towards their own keeping places or museums for storage. This allows the remains to be on home territory and to allow access to the remains should the community wish this in the future.

The use of museums and keeping places run by or for indigenous peoples may have different roles. A keeping place is likely to be a separate space within a museum or cultural centre or as a standalone entity which is concerned primarily with ensuring the safety, security and respectful treatment of the human remains held there. The keeping place and the remains within it are under the control of the related community. Many different groups in either the home country or the state may use the same space but each different group of remains will be separately controlled.

Indigenous museums are another option. These may range from cultural centres to full-scale museums. The remains would be stored there but are more likely to be accessible for research. To be genuinely indigenous they should be under the control of the relevant community, who may employ non-indigenous experts to provide advice. As educational opportunities increase for indigenous peoples these experts may be from their own clan, tribe or nation.

10.5   Keeping Places

Keeping places are usually established either within an existing museum or cultural centre or as a stand-alone storage facility. The idea of keeping places was first proposed for the storage of poorly provenanced remains which might be from the claimant country or a region within the country, but did not have any more information about the origin of the remains than this (Simpson, 2001). In some countries all indigenous remains are kept in these special spaces to show respect. In New Zealand all Maori are kept in keeping places called Wahi tapu. Other remains are also sometimes kept in these special spaces.

More recently keeping places have been proposed as longer-term storage for well provenanced remains under a variety of scenarios. These can range from problems relating to reburial itself, to a wish to think more about the use that the remains might be to the community itself. Reburial can be an expensive business and although many communities wish to rebury they may wish to have the remains on their home territory, in a region associated with the clan, tribe or nation involved. Keeping places ensure that the community involved has control of access to the remains and make all decisions about their disposition and treatment (Simpson, 2001).

However, given the high cost of reburial (Cubillo, 2010) and an increasing number of traditional peoples who are now archaeologists, physical anthropologists or anatomists with an interest in undertaking research on their own people, it is the issue of control of the remains that has become important to many groups. Even if many still feel that they are not ready to do such research, they would like to preserve remains in such a way that they may be accessible in future. There is also a growing understanding that such research can benefit the community itself. In other cases the use of the data collected during the repatriation process can stand in for the remains themselves, particularly when this has been an extensive exercise. Again it is the issue of who controls access to this data and increasingly this is passed to the communities.

A wide variety of keeping places are used. These may be within a museum. In the simplest form this may be an area of the main store which is separated off to store remains returned during repatriation, or it may be a separate space within the store which has been specially constructed. Examples of this are at the National Museum in Canberra Australia and the Brisbane Museum in Queensland. Some communities have developed their own keeping places on traditional lands. Pickering (2002) has set out a variety of methods and types of storage which would be functional but low-cost options. This latter method gives the community total control without any intermediary but it does mean that the community has full responsibility and possibly little backup. This may be a good option for communities who do not want to rebury but who want the remains to be sited on their own lands.

These methods do not have to be applied only to remains from former colonial countries, but can be used for keeping remains in many different situations. The Church of England is exploring the use of disused churches to store human remains excavated from graveyards and church crypts as an alternative to either reburial or cremation. The remains are kept on consecrated ground, as the original burials were, but the care of the remains is with either a local museum or a national body such as Historic England. This approach has already been used successfully in two cases. One is the remains exhumed from the crypt at St Brides, Fleet Street in London. These known individuals are stored in part of the crypt of the church in one of the areas originally used for burials (Mays, 2013). This area is also set out to allow research to take place and is administered by the Museum of London, which is a short walk away. The other is at St Peter's Church, Barton upon Humber. Here the excavated remains from the church and surrounding graveyard are stored in the now redundant church of St Peter's (Mays, 2013). Access to the remains is arranged through the local office of English Heritage and the remains have already been used in a wide variety of research.

Keeping places are a good way of storing remains, giving control to the claimant community once remains are returned to the country of origin. They can be seen as a half-way house arrangement allowing remains to be on 'home' territory but without the problems inherent in reburial both in expense and conflict within the community (see Chapter 7 for fuller discussion).

Dedicated Storage Places within Existing Museums

When human remains are returned it is not uncommon for them to be stored in either the country's national museum or in the state museum of the region where the community making the request holds their traditional territory (Pickering, 2002). These museums have often set up separate storage areas either within the museum or in one of the off-site storage areas. A curator is usually given responsibility for this, which, depending on the museum, might be a dedicated member of staff or an existing curator. Responsibility might be devolved to any unit within the museum that has responsibility for repatriation, particularly for international cases such as in New Zealand at Te Papa Tongarewa Museum. In the case of Te Papa the storage area is a specially consecrated store where the museum staff house and care for the remains until they can be returned to their community. They also have a ceremonial route into the museum along which the remains are carried and enter through a ceremonial gateway (Figure 10.1). Other New Zealand museums have such stores to hold remains from local and national museums in New Zealand.

Figure 10.1 Ceremonial Gateway at Te Papa Tongarewa Museum New Zealand.
Credit: MARTY MELVILLE/Stringer/AFP/Getty Images

Other museums are also trying this approach. The human remains from the Torres Strait Islands for which return was agreed but which the islanders wanted left at the NHM pending further investigations are stored separately within the NHM store. No access is permitted without TSI approval but the remains are conserved by the NHM. Should this be successful then the museum may explore ways of using similar situations for remains from elsewhere in the world, particularly for regions that would like to repatriate but for which this is not a viable option due to lack of funds.

The most important aspect of this is that the remains in all cases are held in trust by the museum, not forming part of their collection but cared for on behalf of the descendant community. All access is undertaken only with the agreement of the community. This approach can also be used for remains from within a country. For example, the NHM is in discussions with the Diocese of London regarding the human remains from Christ Church, Spitalfields to set up a dedicated and consecrated store for the remains. This would allow research access to continue whilst the remains of these identifiable individuals would be held in a similar environment to the original burials.

10.6   Dedicated Museums

The growth of interest around the work in traditional knowledge and cultures make dedicated museums of particular interest to indigenous communities. Collecting their cultural heritage together and displaying it with their own knowledge and reverence can provide a way of showing the world how the community views itself and the world around it (Cubillo, 2010). This also provides a degree of control over how material is presented.

The museums could be of two types. One is set up by the government or other body and may work with communities to develop exhibitions and the methods of presenting and storing both artefacts and remains. The National Museums in both Australia and New Zealand work on such premises. The Museum of the American Indian is another example. It was founded by the government in the United States but as part of an independent institution, the Smithsonian. This museum was in part set up to provide a better understanding of Native American culture but also to help facilitate the repatriation of human remains. It therefore has a different focus from the Australian and New Zealand museums which, although in one case they are mandated to find overseas ancestral remains, act as repositories for human remains that have been returned. Although any remains held in such specially desig-nated museums are under the control of the communities from which they originated, it is unusual for all the staff to be indigenous, though this is changing. The Te Papa Repatriation Unit is a good example, having gone from only 25 per cent indigenous in 2006 to 100 per cent in 2011.

The other type of museum is developed purely through the instigation of the indigenous community either as a nationwide museum or a local museum dealing only with one region or community. These museums grow out of the desire of the community to present their culture them-selves and to pass this on to future generations. One model used for this is the Gabi Tuawi Cultural Centre in Torres Strait, which is an excellent example (Figure 10.2). It was set up with government money but under the control of the local council for the Torres Strait, all of whose councillors are Torres Strait Islanders. It presents the cultural past of the islands through artefacts, films, photographs and modern displays as well as the

Figure 10.2 Gabi Tuawi Cultural Centre, Thursday Island Torres Strait.
© The Trustees of the Natural History Museum London

work of local artists. This then brings together the past, present and future, in the form of education, for the community.

Another model is the museum and tourist centre, such as that at Lake Mungo in Australia. This museum houses very ancient human remains found in the area and returned by the Australian National Museum to the local community. The museum focuses on the long history of the Australian Aboriginal people in Australia but also shows an appreciation that the remains from so long ago are of wider importance, interest and value than just to themselves. Limited research is also allowed and this has provided much information about the early Australians and their likely origin and migrations.

The idea of incorporating human remains within this is logical and, even if they are not displayed, can provide information about the past. As shown above, this is already done in limited way but could be expanded. These museums also provide much-needed employment in traditional areas and draw back those members of the community who have left to undertake academic qualifications.

10.7   Museums and Keeping Places: Taking a Pragmatic Approach

Many communities think that taking physical control means building and running a museum. While this might be possible in some cases, especially for internationally or nationally important remains such as the Lake Mungo remains, it is often outside the scope of the home government's commitment to returning remains 'home'. It is an option to be explored but not something that is a given. However, many communities already have cultural centres and these might be a good model for future retention of remains when the money to rebury is not available or when the community feel that they would like to retain the remains even if not allowing any access. They would be available for the future should they be needed. Any access should always be at the behest of the community or communities. It may be that initially only research benefiting indigenous people would be allowed.

10.8   Conclusions

Repatriation and reburial are not synonymous. Even repatriation may not necessarily mean moving remains to a different institution but could involve simply transferring control from the holding institution to the community requesting return. The most important issue is who controls all matters surrounding access, research and storage of the remains. More usually remains are sent back to the country of origin, and a variety of options are available to ensure the safety and dignity of the remains. This may mean reburial, even if after a long space of time, or it may mean long-term storage in a manner decided by the relevant community. The main issue is that the community has control of the remains and makes the decisions.

Questions

1 Repatriation always means reburial.
   True
   False

2 What is the most important issue to communities when asking for the return of human remains?
   A Return to home country
   B Control of what happens to remains
   C Reburial
   D Responsibility to ancestors

3 How has wider knowledge of forensic techniques aided in their use in repatriation?

4 Which two purposes are keeping places useful for?
   A Storage of poorly provenanced remains
   B Respect for remains
   C Allow access to remains
   D Repatriated remains are under the control of related community

5 Keeping places are exclusively for indigenous remains.
   True
   False

6 Why might indigenous communities want to use keeping places?
   A Store remains while deciding whether to rebury
   B Store remains until more information on origin
   C Have ancestors close to home without reburial
   D Allow access for permitted research
   E All of the above

7 What types of indigenous museums are there?

11 Where Do We Go from Here?

One of the most important concerns to emerge from the repatriation process is that of mutual respect. When each party to a return takes the time and effort needed to begin an understanding of the other's perspective and worldview and getting to know each other, cooperation and collaboration can flow from this. Rather than seeing each other as opposing sides there needs to be an acknowledgement that both want to care for and provide dignity and respect for the human remains that are to be returned. Some institutions have had this collaboration with indigenous communities at their heart for many years; others are only just beginning this journey. There is a need to build on what is already going on so that cooperation between scientists and researchers and the communities becomes the norm rather than an exception which is lauded as something unique and special.

The United Nations Declaration of the Rights of Indigenous People (2008) should be kept in mind when planning any form of collaboration. The declaration covers many aspects of life and interaction with the state. In terms of culture it sets out the right of indigenous people to maintain, control, protect and develop their cultural heritage, traditional knowledge and traditional cultural expressions and states that governments have a responsibility to take effective measures to recognise and protect these rights in conjunction with indigenous people. The later phase, 'in conjunction with indigenous people', is most important as this sets out the equal partnership that indigenous people are provided under the declaration to decide with their government on protecting these rights.

Collaborations between researchers and communities do not have to be expensive or time-consuming once a relationship has been built up. Effort is needed at the outset to build trust and respect between the groups, but it can be done. The NHM staff and the TSI traditional owners built a large amount of respect for each other and a mutual understanding of each other's position. This was hard, as one could say that the NHM had been viewed as the museum that liked to say no! The negative response was actually because the museum was unable by law to return the human remains from any region. Any item once part of the collection, regardless of what it was, could not be removed except under circumstances that did not apply to human remains (see Chapters 3 and 7 for more details). However, the NHM managed to host training opportunities for indigenous Australians which led to progress, from demonstrations on the steps to an impromptu concert by the TSI representatives on the day of the return. This brought the visitors in the museum to a standstill and rang the rafters with applause. To further demonstrate how good relationships can also last, in 2016 the Australian organisers of a session at the World Archaeology Congress to be held in Japan invited me and one of the Torres Strait Traditional Owners, Ned David, to present a joint paper on our experiences of the TSI repatriation. Although a personal issue made it impossible for me to attend, Ned offered to present my part of the paper and did so to great success – something that would have been unthinkable even a few years before.

Once mutual trust and respect are established, the range of collaboration is large. This could include the indigenous community acting as advisor on traditional matters for museum exhibitions on their community. There might also be joint projects and grant applications to improve understanding of repatriation from both perspectives, and molecular analysis, where the community not only would give informed consent and also act in a liaison capacity working as part of the larger team. Another area would be collaboration with museums and companies in terms of traditional knowledge, be this on human remains or more widely in plant and environmental knowledge. However, in this latter case the community would need to be fully engaged and obtain real benefit from any research, through improved health or monetary benefit.

Educational and training opportunities can also be extended, especially if this is seen as mutually beneficial. Many governments in countries such as the United States, Australia and New Zealand have special programmes for giving educational opportunities to indigenous people past the official school-leaving age. Some also provide support so that people can finish standard schooling. Other institutions can offer opportunities in particular at postgraduate level or as training for school leavers or for people working in the heritage and cultural sectors who might not have had the advantage of such training. Several institutions in the home country of the indigenous groups most active in repatriation have training programmes in place. There is also the possibility that these could be extended through cooperation with museums and universities overseas. An exchange programme might bring students in a variety of disciplines together and give them the opportunity to see the world from the perspective of another culture. Museums could partner with other, overseas museums and allow people at the beginning of their career, and later, the opportunity to see a different perspective by using each other's training programmes in a similar way to university exchanges. This would also work for permanent staff, especially from museums in European countries, which often don't have a local indigenous community in the sense the United States, Australia and New Zealand do, as the Europeans are both the dominant culture and the indigenous population. The experience at the NHM and other institutions of even short-term exchanges and extended visits can change and enhance how human remains are perceived.

Cowell and Ferguson (2008) make the point that collaboration is a spectrum, with resistance and no collaboration at one end, participation in the middle and the other end being full and equal partnership. In the literature, the term collaboration often needs to be examined carefully to disentangle what the author means by it, as anything along this spectrum can be described as collaborative if any discussion has taken place. Involvement is essential and should be considered part of ethical practice, research, planning or any activity involving indigenous culture, which should aim to make the community partners rather than subjects (Clegg, 2013b; Carr-Locke, 2015).

One area which could be problematic is in making adjustments to museum practice. All aspects of museum practice are subject to traditional museology. This directs a particular way of caring for and curating objects including human remains. The object is to conserve the remains for the future and to assist in expanding knowledge. Indigenous peoples also have knowledge and traditions in caring for human remains. However, this is wider than purely the remains themselves. To understand the importance of ancestral remains to indigenous people one must first understand the current community. Wide-ranging discussion about all aspects of life is therefore essential if this understanding is to be gained. This is also true in the other direction in that there are often misunderstandings about how museums work and about traditional culture in Western society, despite this often being the dominant culture in the community's home country.

The fellowships hosted at the NHM in 2011 are one example of how working together as equals is important in changing perceptions on both sides. The fellowship holders came to the NHM as members of staff in the same way as anyone else holding a fellowship from the museum would do. They brought with them their knowledge of their own community's ways of dealing with death, and the dead. They shared these insights with the museum staff and helped to inform changes that could be made for Australian remains.

However, new ways of working should not only involve those tradition- ally thought of as indigenous. Within any country there are a range of perspectives on how museums and other institutions should use, exhibit and otherwise give access to remains. When conducting research, particu- larly when remains are relatively modern, one should take account of the views of those related to the people whose remains are to be used as well as local people and special interest groups. This may make research more time-consuming but has the potential to improve the quality of the results of research rather than diminishing it (Clegg *et* al., 2013a). However, it is important that those involved in any consultation about research on any group of human remains and give their consent are genuinely connected to those past populations. It will be a slow process, requiring much effort, patience and goodwill to achieve a new understanding. It means that, to avoid a dialogue of the deaf, as has happened in the past, we all must listen to each other rather than speaking at each other.

Displays of human remains are of great interest to most museum visitors. Working with indigenous communities and others to decide how to present such exhibitions can only add to the experience for the visitor. Information which may not seem important to the museum staff may, when properly explained, be vital to the interpretation of the remains. When people feel they are partners in a venture and are not asked as an afterthought or not at all, then real engagement and cooperation can begin.

We have also as a sector been rather self-deprecating in what we do. This has led to some of the situations we have found encountered in the past. A good example is the view of the Working Group on Human Remains in the United Kingdom (DCMS, 2003). They expressed views about how museums worked without reference to those who did the work. We, in part, allowed this to happen, first by not engaging beyond the formal submission of opinion by various groups and institutions and then by hiding behind the scientific importance of the remains, as if this was the only matter at issue. We should have extended invitations to the working group to visit us at work in all areas from museums to field sites so that the members of the group could see first-hand what we did. In an ideal world the working group would have come to us, but we missed an opportunity. We need to be more proactive and engage with all parts of the wider community, be they local groups, government departments, the legal profession or indigenous communities.

We must not be afraid to talk to different communities about what we do, through public engagement but also by engaging with the media and, as is now happening, posting on social media. We are experts in our field but this does not mean we should have the final say in decisions about what happens to human remains. We should become one part of any process involving remains, giving our opinion fully and frankly remembering that an ethical approach, for example as set out in DCMS Guidance (2004) also means taking account of science. Only once the view that 'we know best' has been shed can true collaboration take place. It may be harder work but the results can be rewarding. It is a much pleasanter place than the past of confrontation and distress. It means acknowledging the humanity of those we may disagree with and being prepared to become an equal partner in all aspects of human remains.

Questions

1 Should repatriation be a quick process?
   Yes
   No

2 What factor is important to a successful repatriation process?
   A Mutual trust
   B Collaboration
   C Discussion

3 Is collaboration an either/or situation?
   Yes
   No

4 What would be the 'gold standard' collaboration?

5 What benefits do indigenous people gain from collaboration with
   scientific or other institutions?
   A Educational
   B Training
   C Collaboration and participation in research
   D No benefit

6 Collaboration means moving from 'doing to' to working with.
   True
   False

7 How can information from communities assist museums?

8 Why should museums be more open and explain more about what
   they do?
   A Makes them more welcoming
   B Dispels misapprehensions
   C No need to be open
   D Carry on as always

9 What is the major belief on the part of scientists and academics that
   must be shed if collaboration is to work?

Answers

Chapter 1

1 B
2 A
3 C
4 Should include:
  Basis for modern collections
  Idea of collecting human remains for museums came from them
5 A, B, C
6 Could include:
  Relics
  Interesting cases
  Education
  Trophies
  Interesting remains
7 D

Chapter 2

1 D
2 A, B
3 Can help with provenance
  Information about the person as an individual (age/sex)
4 F
5 E
6 A, B

Chapter 3

1 E
2 B

3 B, C
4 B
5 C
6 C
7 B
8 B
9 B
10 B

Chapter 4

1 A
2 No
3 Consent from the person who donates their body
4 False
5 Have different legal status and therefore different requirements
6 E
7 Use examples which show how the age of remains alters e.g. Egyptian exhibition in New Zealand
8 False
9 A, B, D
10 Medical; Ethics panel

Chapter 5

1 A
2 A
3 A
4 E
5 Access, storage, acquisitions, documentation, disposal, repatriation, research, including destructive testing and media and images
6 G
7 A, B
8 E
9 A

Chapter 6

1 B
2 A, B
3 B, C
4 Change in position in the store;
   Inclusion of object such as ochre
5 A, C
6 B
7 D
8 If both sides not talking them misunderstandings arise;
   Talking brings about mutual trust if handled well

Chapter 7

1 Yes
2 A, B, E
3 False
4 A
5 True
6 B
7 State
8 B
9 B

Chapter 8

1 Legacy from the past, either from colonial times or by transfer from
   other institutions
2 B
3 C
4 B
5 D
6 Engagement by NHM with community;
   Long timeline for return;
   Ensured remains were from TSI

7 D
8 No funding
  Focus on internal returns
9 B
10 A, C

Chapter 9

1 E
2 D
3 C
4 More
5 A, B, D
6 Makes it easier to exchange information on transfer or allowing information to be comparable when repatriation occurs
7 B
8 D
9 B, C
10 The more is known about remains the better they can fit research

Chapter 10

1 False
2 B, D
3 Greater understanding of terms used and feeling that this is not for benefit of science but to help return identity
4 A, D
5 False
6 E
7 Keeping places in existing museums, cultural centres and standalone museums

Chapter 11

1 No
2 A

3 No
4 Driven by communities and experts as facilitators working as equal
  partners
5 A, B, C
6 True
7 Traditional practices can be matched with signs on remains;
  Information about burials/mortuary practices also aids
8 A, B
9 'We know best'

References

AIJA (Australian Institute of Judicial Administration). 2013. Aspects of Traditional Aboriginal Culture AIJA Aboriginal Cultural Awareness *Benchbook for Western Australian Courts*. Government of Western Australia, Perth.

Airy, G. B. 1881. *Account of Observations of the Transit of Venus, 1874, December 8*, Made under the Authority of the British Government: And of the Reduction of the Observations.

AlQahtani, S. J., Hector, M. P., Livesidge, H. M. 2010. Brief Communication: The London Atlas of Human Tooth Development and Eruption. *American Journal of Physical Anthropology* 142:3.

Anatomy Act. 1832. www.kingscollections.org/exhibitions/specialcollections/charles-dickens-2/italian-boy/anatomy-act

Andrews, C. 1984. *Egyptian Mummies*. Published for the Trustees of the British Museum by British Museum Publications, London.

Arsuaga, J. L., Martinez, I., Gracia, A., Lorenzo, C. 1997. Sima de los Huesos Crania (Sierra de Atapuerca Spain): A Comparative Study. *Journal of Human Evolution* 33(1–2):219–281.

Aufderheide, A. C. 2002. *The Scientific Study of Mummies*. Cambridge University Press, Cambridge.

Auger, E. E. 2005. *The Way of the Inuit Art: Aesthetics and History in and beyond the Arctic*. McFarland & Company, Raleigh, NC.

Australian Federal Government. 2006. Report on Federal Government Repatriation Policy. www.loc.gov/law/help/repatriation-human-remains/australia.php#_ftn7

BABAO. 2003. Submission to the Working Group on Human Remains. www.babao.org.uk/publications/babao-documents/

BABAO. 2016. Code of Ethics. www.babao.org.uk/assets/Uploads-to-Web/code-of-ethics.pdf

Barrett, S. M. 1906. *Geronimo's Story of His Life*. Duffield & Company, New York.

BBC News. 2001. Organ Scandal Background. news.bbc.co.uk/1/hi/1136723.stm

BBC News. 2009. Dutch to Return King's Head. news.bbc.co.uk/1/hi/world/africa/7955997.stm

BBC News. 2011. Germany Returns Namibian Skulls Taken in Colonial Era. www.bbc.co.uk/news/world-europe-15127992

Beete Jukes, J. 1847. *Narrative of the Survey Voyage of HMS Fly.* T. & W. Boone, London.

Bello, S. M., Saladié, P., Cáceres, I., Rodríguez-Hidalgo, A., Parfitt, S. A. 2015. Upper Palaeolithic Ritualistic Cannibalism at Gough's Cave (Somerset, UK): The Human Remains from Head to Toe. *Journal of Human Evolution* 82:170–189.

Bennett, T. 2004. *Pasts beyond Memory: Evolution, Museums, Colonialism.* Routledge, Taylor & Francis Group, London.

Berger, T., Trinkaus, E. 1995. Patterns of Trauma among the Neandertals. *Journal of Archaeological Science* 22:841–852.

Bieder, R. E. 2000. The Representation of Indian Bodies in 19th Century American Anthropology. In *Repatriation Reader: Who Owns Native American Remains?* Mihesuah, D. (ed.). University of Nebraska, Lincoln.

Bin-Salik, M. A. 2007. Text of Invited Lecture on Aboriginal World-view. Australian High Commission, London.

Birch, D. 2009. *The Lollards: The Oxford Companion to English Literature.* 7th edn. Oxford University Press, Oxford

Blackburn, S. 2001. *Ethics: A Very Short Introduction.* Oxford University Press, Oxford.

Bonney, H., Clegg, M. 2011. Heads as Memorials and Status Symbols: The Collection and Use of Skulls in the Torres Strait Islands. In *The Bioarchaeology of the Human Head: Decapitation, Decoration and Deformation.* Bonogofsky, M. (ed.). University Press of Florida, Gainsville.

Brickley, M., Mckinley, J. I. 2004. *Guidelines to the Standards for Recording Human Remains.* BABAO & IFA, Southampton & Reading.

Brighton and Hove Museum. 2005. http://brightonmuseums.co.uk/wp-content/uploads/2014/09/Note-on-return-of-Indigenous-Australian-Human-Remains2009.pdf

Brothwell, D. R. 1972. *Digging Up Bones.* Trustees of the British Museum, London.

Brothwell, D. R. 2004. www.york.ac.uk/news-and-events/news/2004/remains-repatriation/

Browne, J. P. 1846. Memoir of the Late Mr James De Ville. *Phrenological Journal* 19:329–344.

Buckley, H. R., Petchey, P. 2018. Human Remains and Bioarchaeology in New Zealand. In *Human Remains: Legacies of Imperialism, Communism and Colonialism*. O'Donnabhain, B., Lozada, M. C. (eds). Springer International Publishing, Cham.

Buikstra, J. E., Ubelaker, D. H. 1994. Standards for Data Collection from Human Skeletal Remains. *Proceedings of a Seminar at the Field Museum of Natural History*. Arkansas Archeological Report Research Series No. 44. Arkansas Archeological Survey.

Burial Act. 1857. www.legislation.gov.uk/ukpga/Vict/20-21/81/contents

Cambridgeshire County Council. 2009. www.babao.org.uk/assets/Uploads-to-Web/cambridge-hsr-survey.pdf

Carr-Locke, S. 2015. Indigenous Heritage and Public Museums: Exploring Collaboration and Exhibition in Canada and the United States. PhD thesis, Simon Fraser University, Canada.

Chambers, N. 2007. *Scientific Correspondence of Sir Joseph Banks 1765–1820*. Pickering & Chatto. London.

Chartered Institute for Archaeologists. 2015. *Professional Archaeology: A Guide for Clients*. www.archaeologists.net/sites/default/files/CIfA-Client-Guide-low-res.pdf

Clarysse, W. 2011. Egyptian Religion and Magic in the Papyri. In *The Oxford Handbook of Papyrology*. Bagnall, R. S. (ed.). Oxford University Press, Oxford.

Christie, A. 1977. *Agatha Christie: An Autobiography*. Collins, London.

Clegg, M. 2009. The Problem of Provenance: Inaccuracies, Changes and Misconceptions. In *Proceedings of the Ninth Annual Conference of the British Association for Biological Anthropology and Osteoarchaeology*. Lewis, M., Clegg, M. (eds). British Archaeological Reports Archaeopress, Oxford.

Clegg, M. 2011. *Reading the Bones Evolve Magazine*. Summer edn. Natural History Museum, London.

Clegg, M. 2013a. A Change in Perspective: The Impact of Legislative Changes in the UK. In *Global Ancestors: Understanding the Shared Humanity of Our Ancestors*. Clegg, M., Redfern, R., Bekvalac, J., Bonney, H. (eds). Oxbow Books, Oxford.

Clegg, M. 2013b. Conclusions and Ways Forward. In *Curating Human Remains: Caring for the Dead in the United Kingdom*. Giesen, M. (ed.). Boydell & Brewer, Woodbridge.

Clegg, M., Long, S. 2015. The Natural History Museum and Human Remains. In *Heritage, Ancestry and Law: Principles, Policies and Practices in*

Dealing with Historical Human Remains. Redmond-Cooper, R. (ed.). Institute for Art and Law, London.

Clements, A., Hillson, S., De la Torre, I. 2008. Tooth Use in Aboriginal Australia. *Archaeology International* 11:37–40.

Collections Trust. 2018. Spectrum 5 Documentation. https://collectionstrust .org.uk/spectrum/

Colwell, C., Ferguson, T. J. 2017. Tree-Ring Dates and Navajo Settlement Patterns in Arizona. *American Antiquity* 82(1):25–49.

Cubillo, F. 2010. Repatriating Our Ancestors: Who Will Speak for the Dead? In *The Long Way Home: The Meaning and Values of Repatriation*. Turnbull, P., Pickering, M. (eds). Berghahn Books, New York.

Cunliffe, B. 1988. Celtic Death Rituals. *Archaeology* 41(2):39–43.

Cunningham, A. 1997. *The Anatomical Renaissance: The Resurrection of Anatomical Projects of the Ancients*. Scolar Press, Aldershot.

Daniell, C. 1997. *Death and Burial in Medieval England 1066–1550*. Routledge, London.

Davis, J. B. 1867. *Thesaurus Craniorum: Catalogue of the Skulls of the Various Races of Man*. Printed for the subscribers, London.

Day, J. 2006. *The Mummy's Curse: Mummy Mania in the English-Speaking World*. Routledge, London.

DCMS (Department of Culture, Media and Sport). 2003. Report from the Working Group on Human Remains. https://webarchive.nationalarchives .gov.uk/20070205171434/http://www.culture.gov.uk/Reference_library/ Publications/archive_2003/wgur_report2003.htm?contextId={A8126671-C4CD-41D5-9274-7887DB820412}

DCMS (Department of Culture, Media and Sport). 2004. Guidance for the Care of Human Remains in Museums. https://webarchive.nationalarchives.gov .uk/20080308033623/http://www.culture.gov.uk/www.culture.gov.uk/Tem plates/Publishing/PressNotice.aspx?NRMODE=Published&NRNODE GUID=%7bC6210C8C-6935-4767-99BB-F93FB0B476CD%7d&NROR IGINALURL=%2fReference_library%2fPress_notices%2farchive_ 2005%2fdcms126_05%2ehtm%3ftextOnly%3dFalse%26contextId%3d %7b19531B8C-5B34-46BE-B43D-E4E4185ABA91%7d&NRCACHE HINT=NoModifyGuest&contextId=%7B19531B8C-5B34-46BE-B43D-E4E4185ABA91%7D&textOnly=False

Dirkmaat, D. C. 2015. *Companion to Forensic Anthropology*. Wiley Blackwell, Chichester.

Dittmar, J. M., Mitchell, P. D. 2016. From Cradle to Grave via the Dissecting Room: The Role of Foetal and Infant Bodies in Anatomical Education from the Late 1700s to Early 1900. *Journal of Anatomy* 229(6):713–722.

Dorland, S. 2009. The Importance of Squier and Davis' Ancient Monuments of the Mississippi Valley to the Modern Archaeological Approach. *Undergraduate Journal of Anthropology* 1:79–86.

Eire, C. M. N. 1986. *War against the Idols: The Reformation of Worship from Erasmus to Calvin.* Cambridge University Press, Cambridge.

Ferguson, T. J., Anyon, R., Ladd, E. J. 1996. Repatriation at the Pueblo of Zuni: Diverse Solutions to Complex Problems. *American Indian Quarterly* 20(2):251–273.

Fforde, C. 2004. *Collecting the Dead: Archaeology and the Reburial Issue.* Duckworth, London.

Fforde, C., Hubert, J. 2006. Indigenous Human Remains and Changing Museum Ideology. In *A Future for Archaeology: The Past in the Present.* Layton, R., Shannon, S., Stone, P. (eds). UCL Press, London.

Fine-Dare, K. S. 2002. *Grave Injustice: The American Indian Repatriation Movement and NAGPRA.* Nebraska University Press, Lincoln.

Flowers, W. H. 1879. *Catalogue of the Specimens Illustrating the Osteology and Dentition of Vertebrated Animals, Recent and Extinct, Contained in the Museum of the Royal College of Surgeons of England.]. Part 1. Vol. 2, Man: Homo sapiens, Linn.* Taylor & Francis, London.

Foley, R. 2003. Science Argues to Keep Bones. BBC News. http://news.bbc.co.uk/1/hi/sci/tech/3032657.stm

Fowler, L., Powers, N. 2006. *Doctors, Dissection and Resurrection Men: Excavations in the 19th-Century Burial Ground of the London Hospital, London.* Museum of London Archaeology, London.

Fullagar, K. 2009. Bennelong in Britain. *Aboriginal History* 33:31–51.

Galligan, B., Roberts, W. 2004. *Australian Citizenship.* Melbourne University Press, Melbourne.

The Guardian. 2000. Britain Pressed to Return Human Remains. www.theguardian.com/uk/2000/jul/05/ewenmacaskill

The Guardian. 2002. Coming Home. www.theguardian.com/education/2002/feb/21/internationaleducationnews.highereducation

The Guardian. 2018. Irish Giant May Finally Get Respectful Burial after 200 Years on Display. www.theguardian.com/science/2018/jun/22/irish-giant-may-finally-get-respectful-burial-after-200-years-on-display

George, A. (trans.). 1999. *Epic of Gilgamesh.* Penguin Classics, London.

Giesen, M., White, L. 2013. International Perspectives towards Human Remains Curation. In *Curating Human Remains: Caring for the Dead in the United Kingdom,* Giesen, M. (ed.). Boydell Press, Woodbridge.

Glyn, E. D. 1981. *Short History of Archaeology.* Thames & Hudson, London.

Haddon, A. C. 1890. The Ethnography of the Western Tribe of the Torres Straits. *Journal of the Anthropological Institute of Great Britain and Ireland* 19:297–440.

Haddon, A. C. 1904. *Sociology, Magic and Religion of the Western Islanders: Reports of the Cambridge Anthropological Expedition to the Torres Straits.* Vol. 5. Cambridge University Press, Cambridge.

Haddon, A. C. 1932. *Head-Hunters: Black, White and Brown.* Abridged edn. Watts, London.

Hasluck, A. 1967. Yagan (?–1833). *Australian Dictionary of Biography.* National Centre of Biography, Australian National University. http://adb.anu.edu.au/biography/yagan-2826/text4053

Hawkins, S. A. 2010. Sir Hans Sloane (1660–1735): His Life and Legacy. *Ulster Medical Journal* 79(1):25–29.

Hillson, S. 1996. *Dental Anthropology.* Cambridge University Press, Cambridge.

Historic England. 2009. Avebury Reburial Request – Results of Consultation. https://historicengland.org.uk/advice/technical-advice/archaeological-science/human-remains-advice/avebury-reburial-results/

Human Tissue Act England and Wales. 2004. www.legislation.gov.uk/ukpga/2004/30/contents

Humphrey, L. T., Dean, M. C., Jeffries, T. E., Penn, M. 2008. Unlocking Evidence of Early Diet from Tooth Enamel. *Proceedings of the National Academy of Sciences* 105(19):6834–6839.

Hurren, E. T. 2012. *Dying for Victorian Medicine: English Anatomy and Its Trade in the Dead Poor c. 1834–1929.* MacMillan, London.

Hurren, E. T. 2016. *Dissecting the Criminal Corpse: Staging Post-Execution Punishment in Early Modern England.* MacMillan, London.

Impey, O. R., MacGregor, A. 2001. *The Origins of Museums: The Cabinet of Curiosities in Sixteenth- and Seventeenth-Century Europe.* House of Stratus, London.

The Independent. 2003. Manchester Museum Returns Aboriginal Remains to Australia. www.independent.co.uk/news/uk/this-britain/manchester-museum-returns-aboriginal-remains-to-australia-98210.html

Janes, R. 2005. *Losing Our Heads: Beheadings in Literature and Culture.* New York University Press, New York.

Jenkins, T. 2008. Dead Bodies: The Changing Treatment of Human Remains in British Museum Collections and Challenges to the Traditional Model of the Museum. *Mortality* 13(2):105–118.

Jones, D. G., Harris, R. J. 1998. Archaeological Human Remains: Scientific, Cultural and Ethical Considerations. *Current Anthropology* 39(2):253–264.

Jones, J., Higham, T., Oldfield, R., Buckley, S. 2014. Evidence for Prehistoric Origins of Egyptian Mummification in Late Neolithic Burials. *PLoS One* 9(8).

Katzenberg, M. A. 2007. Stable Isotope Analysis: A Tool for Studying Past Diet, Demography and Life History. In Bioarchaeology of the Skeleton. 2nd edn. Katzenberg, M. A., Saunders, S. R. (eds). John Wiley, Hoboken, NJ.

Kinaston, R. L., Walter, R. K., Jacomb, C., Brooks, E., Tayles, N., Halcrow, S. E., Stirling, C., Reid, M., Gray, A. R., Spinks, J., Shaw, B., Fyfe, R., Buckley, H. R. 2013. The First New Zealanders: Patterns of Diet and Mobility Revealed through Isotope Analysis. *PloS One* 8(5).

Kroeber, T. 2002. *Ishi in Two Worlds: A Biography of the Last Wild Indian in North America.* University of California Press, Berkeley.

Lahr, M. 2003. Scientists Fight to Save Ancestral Bone Bank. *The Guardian.* www.theguardian.com/uk/2003/sep/28/australia.highereducation

Leach, M., Levy, B. 2014. *Geronimo: Leadership Strategies of an American Warrior.* Simon & Schuster, New York.

Lovell, N. 2007. Repatriation of Human Remains in Alberta Canada. Paper presented at BABAO Annual Conference 2007. www.babao.org.uk/con ferences/babao-annual-conference-2007/

Macgillivay, J. 1852. *Narrative of the Voyage of H.M.S. Rattlesnake.* Vol. 1. T. & W. Boone, London.

Mackenzie Wilson, D. 2002. *The British Museum: A History.* British Museum Press, London.

Márquez-Grant, N., Fibiger, L. 2011. *The Routledge Handbook of Archaeological Human Remains and Legislation: An International Guide to Laws and Practice in the Excavation and Treatment of Archaeological Human Remains.* Routledge, London.

Maschner, H. D. G., Reedy-Maschner, K. L. 2007. Women and the Baubles of Prestige: Trophies of War in the Arctic and Subarctic. In *Taking and Displaying of Human Body Parts as Trophies by Amerindians.* Chacon, R. J., Dye, D. H. (eds). Springer US, New York.

Mays, S. 2000. Age-Dependent Cortical Bone Loss in Women from 18th and Early 19th Century London. *American Journal of Physical Anthropology* 112(3):349–361.

Mays, S. 2013. Curation of Human Remains at St. Peter's Church, Barton-on-Humber, England. In *Curating Human Remains.* Giesen, M. (eds). Boydell Press, Woodbridge.

McFarlane, S. 1888. *Among the Cannibals of New Guinea: Being the Story of the New Guinea Mission of the London Missionary Society.* John Snow & Company, London.

Mcglade, H. 1998. The Repatriation of Yagan: A Story of Manufacturing Dissent. *Law, Text, Culture* 4:245–255.

Meehan, B. 1971. The Form, Distribution and Antiquity of Australian Aboriginal Mortuary Practices. MA thesis, University of Sydney.

Merrett, D. C., Pfeiffer, S. 2000. Maxillary Sinusitis as an Indicator of Respiratory Health in Past Populations. *American Journal of Physical Anthropology* 111(3):301–318.

Mitchell, P. D., Boston, C., Chamberlain, A. T., Chaplin, S., Chauhan, V., Evans, J., Fowler, L., Powers, N., Walker, D., Webb, H., Within, A. 2011. The Study of Anatomy in England from 1700 to the Early 20th Century. *Journal of Anatomy* 219(2):91–99.

Momerie, A., Wilkins, W., Crackanthorpe, H. 1892. *Medieval Medicine. The Albemarle* 2(2):52–56.

Morris, L. 2017. The Last Indigenous Tasmanian. *National Geographic*. www.nationalgeographic.com.au/australia/the-last-indigenous-tasmanian.aspx

Mossier, F. 1996. *Pocahontas: The Life and the Legend*. De Capo Press, New York.

Muinzer, T. 2013. A Grave Situation: An Examination of the Legal Issues Raised by the Life and Death of Charles Byrne, the 'Irish Giant'. *International Journal of Cultural Property* 1:23–48.

National Museum of the American Indian Act. United States Government (NMAIA). 1989. https://americanindian.si.edu/sites/1/files/pdf/about/NMAIAct.pdf

Native American Graves Protection and Repatriation Act (NAGPRA). 1990. www.nps.gov/history/local-law/FHPL_NAGPRA.pdf

New York Times. 1909. Old Apache Chief Geronimo Is Dead. www.nytimes.com/learning/general/onthisday/bday/0616.html

New York Times. 2009. Geronimo's Heirs Sue Secret Yale Society over His Skull. www.nytimes.com/2009/02/20/us/20geronimo.html

New Zealand Government. 1840. Treaty of Waitangi. www.teara.govt.nz/en/treaty-of-waitangi

New Zealand Herald. 2006. Talks Avoid Disrespect to Egyptian Mummy. www.nzherald.co.nz/nz/news/article.cfm?c_id=1&objectid=10413985

Newbury, C. 2001. Patronage and Bureaucracy in the Hawaiian Kingdom, 1840–1893. *Pacific Studies* 24(1–2):1–36.

NHM (Natural History Museum). 2006. NHM Ethics Committee. www.nhm.ac.uk/about-us/governance.html

Ousely, S. D., Billeck, W. T., Hollinger, R. E. 2005. Federal Repatriation Legislation and the Role of Physical Anthropology. *American Journal of Physical Anthropology* 48:2–32.

Palmer, N. 2003. *Chapter One Report of the Working Group on Human Remains*. Department of Culture Media and Sport, HMSO, London.

Pate, F. D., Brodie, R., Owen, T. D. 2002. Determination of Geographic Origin of Unprovenanced Aboriginal Skeletal Remains in South Australia Employing Stable Carbon and Nitrogen Isotope Analysis. *Australian Archaeology* 55:1–7.

Pearson, O. M., Buikstra, J. E. 2009. Bones and Behaviour. In *Bioarchaeology: The Contextual Analysis of Human Remains*. Buikstra, J. E., Beck, L. A. (eds). Routledge, New York.

Peaslee, A. J. 1974. *Constitutions of Nations Vol. III Europe*. Springer, The Hague.

Pickering, M. 2002. Repatriation, Rhetoric, and Reality: The Repatriation of Australian Indigenous Human Remains and Sacred Objects. *Journal of the Australian Registrars Committee* 15–19:40–41.

Pickering, M., Gordon, P. 2011. Repatriation: The End of the Beginning. In *Understanding Museums: Australian Museums and Museology*. Griffin, D., Paroissien, L. (eds). National Museum of Australia. https://nma.gov .au/research/understanding-museums/

Plomley, N. J. B. 1987. *Weep in Silence: A History of the Flinders Island Aboriginal Settlement*. Blubberhead Press, Hobart.

Quigley, C. 2001. *Skulls and Skeletons: Human Bone Collections and Accumulations*. Macfarlane & Co., London.

Qureshi, S. 2004. Displaying Sara Baartman, the 'Hottentot Venus'. *History of Science* 42(2):233–357.

Rasmussen, M., Sikora, M., Albrechtsen, A., Willerslev, E. 2015. The Ancestry and Affiliation of Kennewick Man. *Nature* 523:455–458.

Rawley, J. A., Behrendt, S. D. 1981. *The Transatlantic Slave Trade: A History*. University of Nebraska Press. Lincoln.

Redfern, R., Bekvalac, J. 2013. The Museum of London: An Overview of Policy and Procedures. In *Curating Human Remains: Caring for the Dead in the United Kingdom*. Geisen M. (ed.). Boydell Press. Woodbridge.

Redfern, R., Clegg, M. 2017. Archaeologically Derived Human Remains in England: Legacy and Future. *World Archaeology* 49(5):574–587.

Relief, F. P., Cilliers, L. 2005. Burial Customs and the Pollution of Death in Ancient Rome. *Acta Theologica Supplementum* 7:29–43.

Robb, J., Elster, E. S., Isetti, E., Knüsel, C. J., Tafuri, M. A., Traverso, A. 2015. Cleaning the Dead: Neolithic Ritual Processing of Human Bone at Scaloria Cave, Italy. *Antiquity* 89:39–54.

Roberts, C. 2013. Archaeological Human Remains and Laboratories: Attaining Acceptable Standards for Curating Skeletal Remains for Teaching and

Research. In *Curating Human Remains: Caring for the Dead in the United Kingdom*. Geisen, M. (ed.). Boydell Press, Woodbridge.

Robertson, G. 2007. Losing the Plot. *The Bulletin*, 26 April.

Rogers, C. J. 2011. The Development of the Longbow in Late Medieval England and 'Technological Determinism'. *Journal of Medieval History* 37(3):321–341.

Royal College of Surgeons. 1831. Archives. http://surgicat.rcseng.ac.uk/Details/collect/4123

Royer, K. 2003. The Body in Parts: Reading the Execution Ritual in Late Medieval England. *Historical Reflections / Réflexions Historiques* 29(2):319–339.

Ruckstahl, K., Tayles, N., Buckley, H. R., Bradley, R., Fyfe, R., Ellison, M. 2016. The Ancestors Speak: Kiwi Tangati Matawanga Maori and the Development of Biological Anthropology in New Zealand. In *The Routledge Handbook of Bioarchaeology in Southeast Asia and the Pacific Islands*. Oxenham, M., Buckley, H. R. (eds). Routledge, Oxford.

Rutherford, S. 2008. *The Victorian Cemetery*. Shire Publications, Oxford.

Scarre, G. 2009. The Repatriation of Human Remains. In *The Ethics of Cultural Appropriation*. Young, O. J., Brunk, C. G. (eds). Blackwell, Oxford.

Scheuer, L., Black, S. 2000. *Developmental Juvenile Osteology*. Academic Press, London.

Schrag, B. 1997. With Bones in Contention: Repatriation of Human Remains. *Graduate Research Ethics: Cases and Commentaries. Vol. 1*. Association for Practical and Professional Ethics. www.onlineethics.org/Resources/gradres/gradresv1/bones.aspx

Schrag, B. 2006a. Ethical Considerations with Archaeology and Community Conflict. *Graduate Research Ethics: Cases and Commentaries. Vol. 7*. Association for Practical and Professional Ethics. www.onlineethics.org/Resources/gradres/gradresv7/35091.aspx

Schrag, B. 2006b. The Case of the Overeager Collaborator. *Graduate Research Ethics: Cases and Commentaries. Vol. 7*. Association for Practical and Professional Ethics. www.onlineethics.org/Resources/gradres/gradresv7/35071.aspx

Schultz, L. O., Bennett, P. H., Ravussin, E., Kidd, J. R., Kidd, K. K., Esparza, J., Valencia, M. E. 2006. Effects of Traditional and Western Environments on Prevalence of Type 2 Diabetes in Pima Indians in Mexico and the U.S. *Diabetes Care* 29(8):1866–1871.

Simpson, M. G. 2001. *Making Representations: Museums in the Post-Colonial Era*. Routledge, Abingdon, Oxon.

Smith, B. H. 1991. Standards of Human Tooth Formation and Dental Age Assessment. In *Advances in Dental Anthropology*, Kelley, M. A., Larsen, C. S. (eds). Wiley-Liss, New York.

St. Clair, W. 1998. *Lord Elgin and the Marbles.* 3rd edn. Oxford University Press, New York.

Stanley, N. 2007. *The Future of Indigenous Museums: Perspectives from the South West Pacific.* Berghahn Books, Oxford.

Strand-Vidorsdottir, U., O'Higgins, P., Stringer, C. B. 2002. A Geometric Morphometric Study of Regional Differences in the Ontogeny of the Modern Human Facial Skeleton. *Journal of Anatomy* 201(30):211–229.

Stringer, C. B. 1978. Some Problems in Middle and Upper Pleistocene Hominid Relationships. In *Recent Advances in Primatology.* Vol. 3, *Evolution.* Chivers, D. J., Joysey, K. (eds). Academic Press, London.

Stringer, C. B. 1982. Towards a Solution to the Neanderthal Problem. *Journal of Human Evolution* 11:431–438.

Stringer, C. B. 1985. Middle Pleistocene Hominid Variability and the Origin of Late Pleistocene Humans. In *Ancestors: The Hard Evidence.* Delson, E., Alan R. (eds). Wiley-Liss, New York.

Stringer, C. B. 2003. Bones of Contention. *The Telegraph.* www.telegraph.co.uk/education/3322744/Bones-of-contention.html

Stumpe, L. H. 2005. Stealing History: A Debate about Cultural Property. www.liverpoolmuseums.org.uk/ism/resources/stealing_history_2005.aspx

Summers, M. 1881. The Ascent of Brenchley and Remy to Mauna Loa, Island of Hawaii. *Hawaiian Journal of History* 22:33–69.

Szecsenyi-Nagy, A., Brandt, G., Haak, W., Keerl, V., Jakucs, J., Muller-Rieker, S., Kohler, K., Mende, B. G., Oross, K., Marton, T., Osztas, A., Kiss, V., Fecher, M., Palfi, G., Molner, E., Sebok, K., Czene, A., Paluch, T., Slaus, M., Novak, M., Pecina-Slaus, N., Osz, B., Voicsek, V., Somogyi, K., Toth, G., Kromer, B., Banfty, E., Alt, K. W. 2015. Tracing the Genetic Origin of Europe's First Farmers Reveals Insights into Their Social Organization. *Proceedings of the Royal Society B* 282:20150339.

The Times. 2006. Sending Back Aboriginal Bones Is a Loss to Scientists. www.thetimes.co.uk/article/sending-back-of-aboriginal-bones-is-loss-to-scientists-2m23vlkf8gq

Thomas, O. 1885. Account of a Collection of Skulls from the Torres Straits. *Journal of the Anthropological Institute of Great Britain and Ireland* 14:328–343.

Thompson, T., Errikson, D. 2017. *Another Dimension: The Application of Imaging to the Study of Human Remains.* Academic Press, London.

Toynbee, J. M. C. 1996. *Death and Burial in the Roman World.* Johns Hopkins University Press, Baltimore, MD.

Tyler, H. R. 2014. Gall, Franz Joseph. In *Encyclopedia of the Neurological Sciences.* Aminoff, M. J., Daroff, R. B. (eds). Elsevier, Berlin.

United Nations Declaration on the Rights of Indigenous Peoples. 2007. www
.un.org/development/desa/indigenouspeoples/declaration-on-the-rights-
of-indigenous-peoples.html

Van Wyhe, J. 2004. *Phrenology and the Origins of Victorian Scientific Natur-
alism.* Ashgate, Aldershot.

Vrdoljak, A. F. 2008. Self Determination and Cultural Rights. In *Cultural
Human Rights.* Francioni, F., Scheinin, M. (eds). Brill Nijhoff, Leiden.

Walford, E. 1878. The British Museum: Part 1 of 2. In *Old and New London.*
Vol. 4: 490–519. British History Online. www.british-history.ac.uk/old-
new-london/vol4/pp490-519

Walker, P. L. 2000. Bioarchaeological Ethics: A Historical Perspective on the Value
of Human Remains. In *Bioarchaeology of the Human Skeleton.* 2nd edn.
Katzenberg, M., Anne Saunders Shelley, R. (eds). John Wiley, Hoboken, NJ.

Ward, B. 2010. Relics and the Medieval Mind. *International Journal for the
Study of the Christian Church* 10(4):274–286.

Ward, R. 2015. The Criminal Corpse, Anatomists, and the Criminal Law:
Parliamentary Attempts to Extend the Dissection of Offenders in Late
Eighteenth-Century England. *Journal of British Studies* 54(1):63–87.

Wellcome Trust. Repatriation of Australian Human Remains. https://
wellcome.ac.uk/funding/managing-grant/return-australian-aboriginal-skulls-
wellcome-collections-held-science-museum

White, T. D., Berhane, A., DeGusta, D., Gilbert, H., Richards, G. D., Suwa, G.,
Clark Howell, F. 2003. Homo Sapiens from Middle Awash, *Ethiopia
Nature* 423:742–747.

White, T. D., Black, M. T., Folkens, P. A. 2012. *Human Osteology.* 3rd edn.
Academic Press, London.

Williamson, G. 1857. *Observations on the Human Crania Contained in the
Museum of Army Medical Department, Fort Pitt, Chatham.* Dublin University Press, Dublin.

Wilson, L. A., Macleod, N., Humphrey, L. T. 2008. Morphometric Criteria for
Sexing Juvenile Human Skeletons Using the Ilium. *Journal of Forensic
Sciences* 53(2):269–278.

Woolley, C. L. 1934. *Ur Excavations. Vol II, The Royal Cemetery.* British
Museum, London; University Museum Philadelphia, Philadelphia.

Wypijewski, J. 2006. The Collection and Use of Skulls in the Torres Strait
Islands. *Mother Jones* 31(1):24, 26–27.

Young, G. 1883. *The Voyage of the Wanderer.* MacMillan, London.

Zorich, Z. 2014. Neanderthals Bury Their Dead? *Archaeology* 67(2):19.

Index